The Kingfisher

ILLUSTRATED
HISTORY
—OF·THE—
WORLD

The Kingfisher

ILLUSTRATED

HISTORY

OF·THE

WORLD

VOLUME 10

The Modern World
1950 to Present Day

Kingfisher Books

NEW YORK

Consultant Editor
Professor Jack Zevin

General Editor
Charlotte Evans

Project Designer and Art Editor
Stefan Morris

Project Editors
Annabel Else, Lee Simmons, Nina Hathway, Margaret Younger

Designers and Art Editors
Branka Surla, Jackie Moore, Smiljka Surla

Editorial Manager
Catherine Headlam

Design Manager
Louise Jervis

Picture Research
Elaine Willis, Su Alexander

Contributors
Hazel Martell, Theodore Rowland-Entwistle, Fiona Macdonald,
Ken Hills, Elizabeth Longley, Teresa Chris, Neil Grant, John Paton

Advisers
Ellie Bowden, John Harrop, Robert Guyver

KINGFISHER BOOKS
Grisewood & Dempsey Inc.
95 Madison Avenue
New York, New York 10016

First American edition 1993
2 4 6 8 10 9 7 5 3 1
Copyright © Grisewood & Dempsey Ltd. 1992

Library of Congress Cataloging-in-Publication Data
The Kingfisher illustrated history of the world: 40,000 B.C. to present
day/foreword by Magnus Magnusson: introduction by Jack Zevin: [general editor, Charlotte
Evans: contributors, Hazel Martell . . . et al.]. – 1st American ed.
p.   cm.
Includes index.
Summary: Traces the history of the world, from the ancient world
of 40,000 B.C. to the present day, covering such aspects as war,
society, religion, people, buildings, arts, science, and communication.
1. World history–Juvenile literature. [1. World history.]
I. Evans, Charlotte.   II. Kingfisher Books.
D20.K56   1993
909–dc20   92-29123   CIP   AC

ISBN 1-85697-855-9 (10 volume edition)

Printed in Italy

Contents

The Modern World

The years between 1950 and the present day are recent history and concern people many of whom are still alive. Some of the events may have occurred during our lifetime, or we may have seen them on television. Also social, technological, and environmental changes are taking place all the time. This makes it difficult for historians to select the really important events from the vast amount of information that is available in the modern world. Many of the events that seem important today may not be thought important in fifty or a hundred years from now.

Some events seem too important to leave out. Since 1950 there have been many "firsts." The first astronauts, the first test-tube babies, the first VCRs, and the first personal computers.

There have been major political changes, including independence for many new nations in Africa and other continents, and the breakup of the once-powerful USSR. There have been tragic wars in the Far East and Middle East. Economic power is moving away from Europe and North America toward the Far East.

Politicians and policymakers, as well as historians, have identified several important trends that seem to be transforming our world: the long-term effects of environmental pollution, increasing population, changing family structures, and the growing gap between rich and poor people and countries.

All these concerns have yet to be assessed, but that is the future, not the past.

▼ *Joyful Berliners pull down the wall which overshadowed their lives for nearly 30 years. It was built to prevent the East Germans traveling to the West.*

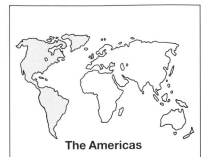

The Americas

1951 First U.S. nuclear power stations.

1959 Revolution in Cuba, Fidel Castro in power.
1962 Cuban missile crisis.
1962–1966 Civil rights protests. Growth of Black power movement.
1963 President Kennedy is assassinated.

1968 Martin Luther King is assassinated.
1969 American astronaut walks on the Moon.
1970 Communist Salvador Allende becomes president of Chile.
1974 President Nixon resigns.
1979 Civil war in Nicaragua and El Salvador.
1981 First U.S. space shuttle flight.
1982 Falklands War.
1983 Argentinean government is overthrown. New democratic leadership.
1987 U.S. signs INF treaty with USSR. They agree to ban all intermediate nuclear weapons.
1988 George Bush is elected president.
1992 Representatives of all nations meet at Earth summit in Rio to discuss future of planet.
1993 Bill Clinton is inaugurated as president.

Europe

1955 Warsaw Pact is signed.
1956 Hungarian Rising is put down by USSR.
1957 Common Market (EEC) is established.

1961 Berlin Wall is built. Russian cosmonaut is first man to orbit in space.
1968 Soviet troops invade Czechoslovakia.
1969 Irish Republican Army (IRA) begins campaign for a united Ireland.
1973 Britain, Ireland, and Denmark join the European Community (EC).
1975 Death of Franco ends dictatorship in Spain.

1980 Polish trade union, Solidarity, is created.
1981 Greece joins EC. IRA hunger strikes in Ireland.
1985 Gorbachev becomes leader of the USSR.
1986 Chernobyl nuclear disaster in Ukraine. Spain and Portugal join EC.
1989 Ceaucescu is overthrown in Romania.
1990 East and West Germany are reunited.
1991 Gorbachev resigns. Communist Party is outlawed in USSR. USSR breaks up. Civil war in Yugoslavia.

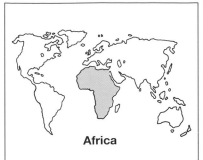

Africa

1952 Mau Mau fighters in Kenya seek independence.
1957 Ghana becomes independent.
1960 Nigeria and Zaire become independent. Sharpeville massacre in South Africa.
1961 Tanzania becomes independent.
1962 Algeria and Uganda become independent.
1963 Kenya becomes independent.
1964 Zambia and Malawi become independent.
1965 White minority government in Rhodesia (now Zimbabwe) declares itself independent from Britain.
1967–1970 Civil war in Nigeria. Many die of starvation in Biafra.
1974 Emperor Haile Selasse of Ethiopia is overthrown by military leaders.
1975 Angola and Mozambique become independent.
1980 Black majority rule is achieved in Zimbabwe.
1986 Fighting in South African townships between rival Black groups.

1990 African National Congress (ANC) leader Nelson Mandela is released from South African prison.

Middle East

Asia and the Far East

Australasia and Pacific

1952 Military takeover in Egypt.
1953 Egypt becomes independent.
1956 Suez Crisis.
1967 Six Day War.

1972 Palestine Liberation Organization (PLO) stages terrorist attacks.
1973 Yom Kippur War.
1973–1974 OPEC countries, led by Arab states, rapidly increase oil prices.
1976–1982 Civil war between Christians and Muslims in Lebanon.
1979 Egypt and Israel sign peace treaty. Shah of Iran is overthrown.
1980–1988 Iran-Iraq War.
1981 President Sadat of Egypt is assassinated.
1982 Israel invades Lebanon.

1986 U.S. bombs Libya.

1990 Iraq invades Kuwait. Soviet troops intervene to try to end ethnic dispute between Armenia and Azerbaijan.
1991 UN forces Iraq to withdraw from Kuwait.

1950–1953 Korean War.

1962 War between India and China.
1963 Malaysia becomes independent.
1964–1975 War in Vietnam.
1965 America sends troops to Vietnam. War between India and Pakistan. Singapore becomes independent.
1966 Cultural Revolution begins in China.
1971 Bangladesh becomes independent.
1973 American troops withdraw from Vietnam.
1975 Communists control Vietnam, Laos, and Cambodia.
1976 Death of Mao Zedong.
1978 Vietnam invades Cambodia.
1979 USSR invades Afghanistan.
1984 Indira Gandhi, Indian prime minister, is assassinated. Agreement between Britain and China that Hong Kong will be returned to China in 1997.

1988–1990 Benazir Bhutto is prime minister of Pakistan.
1989 Demonstrators calling for democracy are attacked by Chinese government troops in Tiananmen Square, Beijing.

1951 ANZUS alliance is signed between Australia, New Zealand, and U.S.
1954 U.S. tests atomic bombs in the Pacific.

1959 Hawaii becomes the 50th state of the U.S.

1966 Australian troops fight alongside Americans in Vietnam.

1972 Labor party victories in general elections in Australia and New Zealand after many years of Conservative rule.
1975 Papua New Guinea becomes independent.

1978 Solomon Islands and Tuvalu become independent.
1985 South Pacific Forum draws up Nuclear Free Zone Treaty. French agents blow up Greenpeace ship *Rainbow Warrior*.

1987 Scientists confirm existence of a hole in the ozone layer above Antarctica.

The World

This period was dominated by the Cold War between communism and the West, in which the **United States** and the **Soviet Union** played the leading parts. These two were also involved in the space race. The USSR was the first to send a man into space, and the United States the first to put a man on the Moon. Changes in the USSR led to the end of the Cold War, but created uncertainty about the future as nationalists demanded independence.

In western **Europe**, the European Community encouraged economic growth and worked toward political union. In **Africa**, many nations became independent, but faced severe economic problems as well as drought and famine. In some countries militant Islamic groups have risen to power causing conflict.

In **Southeast Asia**, industry and technology developed, and Japanese business has become the most successful in the world. **China** experienced a cultural revolution and tried to reduce its population. Indochina (Southeast Asia) was devastated by wars.

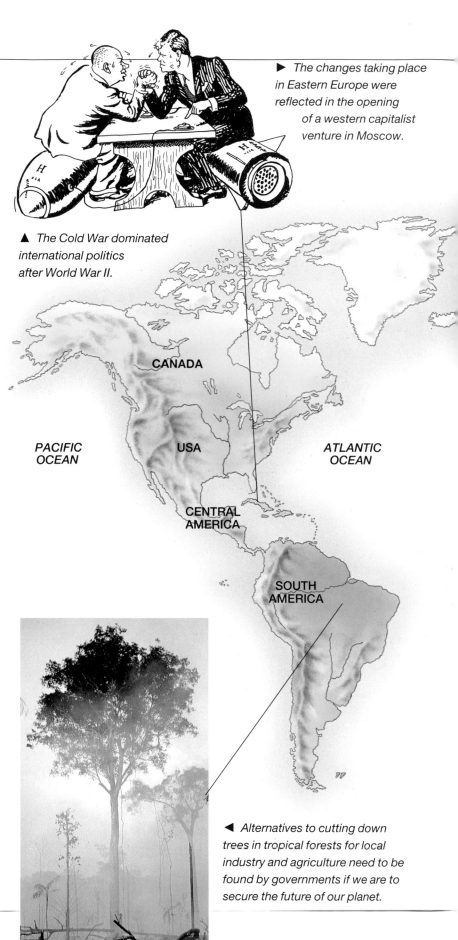

▶ The changes taking place in Eastern Europe were reflected in the opening of a western capitalist venture in Moscow.

▲ The Cold War dominated international politics after World War II.

CANADA

PACIFIC OCEAN

USA

ATLANTIC OCEAN

CENTRAL AMERICA

SOUTH AMERICA

◀ Alternatives to cutting down trees in tropical forests for local industry and agriculture need to be found by governments if we are to secure the future of our planet.

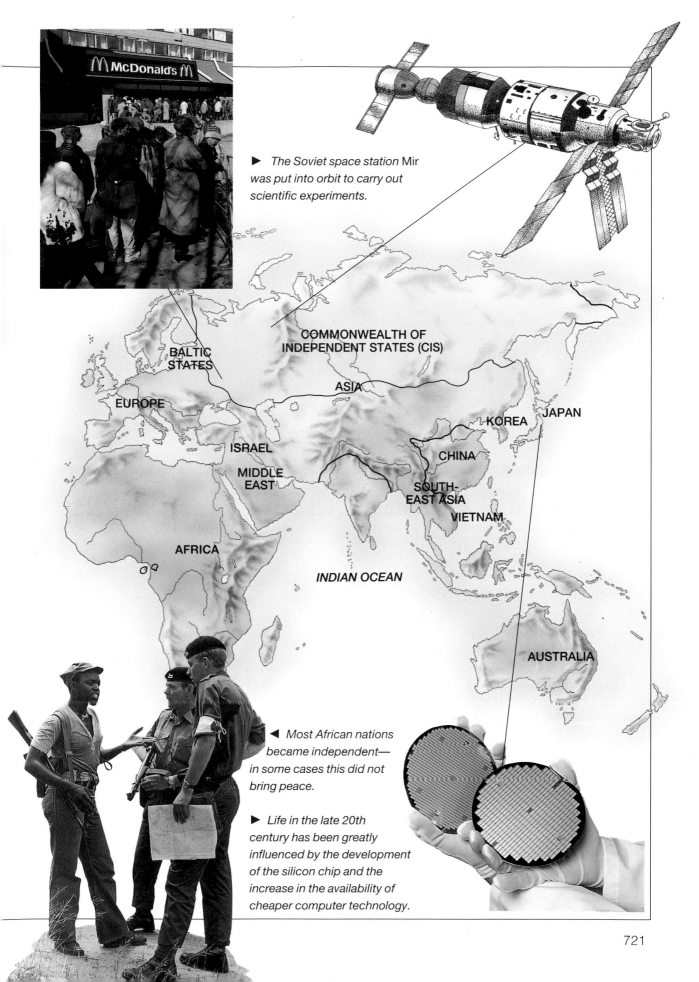

► The Soviet space station Mir was put into orbit to carry out scientific experiments.

COMMONWEALTH OF INDEPENDENT STATES (CIS)

BALTIC STATES

EUROPE

ASIA

KOREA

JAPAN

ISRAEL

MIDDLE EAST

CHINA

SOUTH-EAST ASIA

VIETNAM

AFRICA

INDIAN OCEAN

AUSTRALIA

◄ Most African nations became independent— in some cases this did not bring peace.

► Life in the late 20th century has been greatly influenced by the development of the silicon chip and the increase in the availability of cheaper computer technology.

721

1950 USSR and Communist China sign a 30-year friendship treaty. Korean War: Invasion of South Korea by North Korean forces (to 1953).

1951 ANZUS security treaty is signed by Australia, New Zealand, and U.S. First U.S. nuclear power station built.

One of the first postage stamps to feature the head of the new queen, Elizabeth II, in the first years of her reign.

1952 Britain: Elizabeth II becomes queen. Kenya: Mau Mau terrorist groups seek independence from Britain.

1953 End of the Korean War. U.S.: Dwight D. Eisenhower becomes president (to 1961). USSR: Nikita Khrushchev becomes leader (to 1964). Nepal: Edmund Hilary and Tensing Norgay reach top of Mount Everest. U.S.: Arthur Miller's play *The Crucible* draws parallel between witch hunts and Senator Joseph McCarthy's campaign against alleged Communists. Ernest Hemingway wins Pulitzer Prize for *The Old Man and the Sea*.

1954 France, U.S., USSR, and Britain discuss the future of Germany; USSR insists on a division between east and west Germany. Vietnam: French colonial troops defeated by Communists at Dien Bien Phu. U.S.: Supreme Court rules whites-only schools unlawful. U.S. tests nuclear bombs in Pacific. Egypt: General Nasser elected president (to 1970). Britain: Roger Bannister runs mile (1.6 km) in under four minutes.

1955 West Germany becomes a member of North Atlantic Treaty Organization (NATO). Eastern Europe: Communist countries sign Warsaw Pact. Middle East: Tension increases on Israel-Jordan border. U.S.: Martin Luther King leads civil rights protest.

The Cold War

The USSR and the U.S. fought together as allies in World War II, but in 1945 these two superpowers became enemies. This division became known as the Cold War – a war without fighting. The United States and USSR "fought" by making threats and by strengthening their armed forces. They stockpiled nuclear weapons. Peaceful, friendly contacts between their peoples ceased. The USSR became shut off from the rest of the world. The British statesman Winston Churchill described the frontier between East and West as the "iron curtain."

The Cold War dominated politics for many years. On one side, the United States became leader of NATO (an alliance of Western nations against the communist powers). On the other side, the USSR dominated the Warsaw Pact, a military alliance of East European states that supported communism. When the Hungarians in 1956 and the Czechs in 1968 tried to act independently, Soviet forces were sent in to regain control.

▲ *Rebel guerrillas in Afghanistan fought against government and Soviet troops in the 1980s. They wanted to free their country from Soviet control.*

▶ *Czech students trying to stop Soviet tanks in Prague, in August 1968. The USSR feared that independent actions by Warsaw Pact members might weaken its power, so it moved troops into Czechoslovakia.*

◄ By 1949, most European states had joined rival alliances. Warsaw Pact states supported the USSR. Members of the North Atlantic Treaty Organization (NATO) supported the U.S.A.

▼ A 1962 cartoon shows the two superpower leaders arm-wrestling for power: USSR's Nikita Khrushchev (left) facing the U.S. President John F. Kennedy. They are sitting on nuclear weapons.

Although the U.S. and USSR never fought, they came close to it in 1962 when Soviet missiles were based in Cuba. Both sides have sent money and arms to encourage fighting in Korea, Vietnam, Iraq, Cambodia, Nicaragua, and Afghanistan. In 1969, the two first met to discuss disarmament and by 1987 they had agreed to abolish medium-range nuclear missiles. The Cold War was over.

The Space Race

The development of technology during World War II helped scientists to realize that one day it might be possible for people to travel in space. Cold War rivalry between the United States and the USSR helped the space race to get going. Both sides felt that being the first nation in space would increase their prestige. They also hoped that space science would help them develop new, more powerful weapons.

The Soviets achieved the first "space first" when they sent a satellite into orbit around the world in 1957. Soon both sides were investing enormous amounts of time and money in space science. Notable achievements included the first manned flights, probes sent to the Moon and past Venus, and the launch of weather and communications satellites.

In 1961, President John F. Kennedy said that American scientists would get a man to the Moon by 1970. In fact, United States' astronauts landed on the Moon in 1969. By 1975, five other countries (France, China, Japan, Britain, and India) had launched their own spacecraft in the space race.

More recently, competition between the two superpowers has turned to co-operation, with scientists sharing ideas and inventions. They have concentrated on long-distance, unmanned space probes, designed to investigate distant planets in the solar system, rather than trying to achieve expensive, eye-catching firsts. International cooperation has also helped to produce orbiting space stations where peaceful scientific experiments can be performed under conditions very different from those on Earth.

▲ The first man on the Moon was the American astronaut Neil Armstrong. He described walking on the Moon as "one small step for a man, one giant leap for mankind."

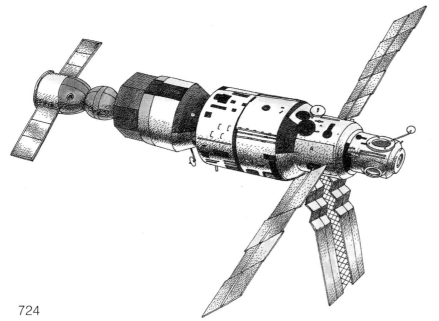

◄ The Soviet space station Mir was launched in 1986. It was designed to stay in orbit for long periods, so that complicated scientific experiments could be carried out on board.

EXPERIMENTS IN SPACE

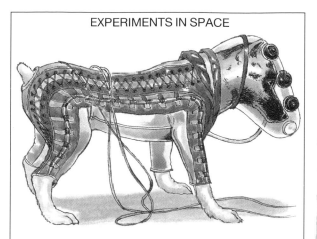

Laika, a Soviet dog, was the first animal in space. She left Earth on November 3, 1957, in a capsule on board *Sputnik 2*. It contained an air supply, food and water, together with instruments for recording her heartbeat, breathing, and blood pressure. They transmitted data back to scientists on Earth. At that time, engineers did not know how to bring a spacecraft safely back to Earth, so sadly Laika died in space. Experiments like these provided vital information for human space travel.

SPACE FIRSTS

1957 USSR launches first satellite, *Sputnik 1*.
1959 *Luna 2* probe (USSR) hits the Moon.
1961 Yuri Gagarin (USSR) is first man in space.
1962 U.S.A. launches first communications satellite.
1963 Valentina Tereshkova (USSR) is first woman cosmonaut.
1969 *Apollo 11* astronauts Neil Armstrong and Edwin Aldrin (U.S.A.) land on the Moon.
1971 USSR sends two probes to Mars.
1975 U.S.A. and USSR cooperate in space; *Apollo* and *Soyuz* craft dock (link) in orbit.
1977 U.S.A. sends *Voyager 2* mission to fly past Jupiter, Saturn, Uranus, and Neptune.
1981 Flight of first space shuttle (U.S.A.).
1983 Flight of first *Spacelab* (U.S.A.).
1986 *Pioneer* spacecraft (U.S.A.) leaves solar system.
1986 Shuttle *Challenger* (U.S.A.) explodes; crew is killed and U.S. shuttle program is delayed.
1990 Hubble Space Telescope (U.S.A.) launched.

1956 Pakistan becomes an Islamic republic. Egypt takes control of Suez Canal which leads to war with France and Britain. Hungary: Soviet troops invade to stop movement toward independence. US.: Segration on buses is declared unconstitutional. Elvis Presley and rock and roll music are popular.
1957 Treaty of Rome sets up European Economic Community (EEC). USSR: Launch of the first space satellite *Sputnik 1*. Italy: Russian author Boris Pasternak publishes his novel *Doctor Zhivago*. U.S.: Riots in Little Rock, Arkansas, over government policy requiring the end of whites-only schools. Composer Leonard Bernstein writes the musical *West Side Story*. Novelist Jack Kerouac publishes *On the Road*.
1958 West Indian Federation is formed to protect trade and political interests. Cuba: Fidel Castro leads a revolution. France: Charles de Gaulle becomes president (to 1969). U.S.: National Aeronautics and Space Administration (NASA) launches first satellite. Marilyn Monroe stars in the film *Some Like It Hot*. Britain: Its first superhighway opens. Dramatist Harold Pinter writes *The Birthday Party*.
1959 USSR launches rocket with monkeys aboard. Canada: St. Lawrence Seaway is opened. Cuba: Castro in power. U.S.: Hawaii becomes 50th state.

The first satellite Sputnik 1 weighed over 183 pounds (83 kg) and carried a radio transmitter.

1960 Nigeria and Zaire become independent. USSR: Soviets shoot down American U-2 spy plane. Egypt: Work starts on Aswan High Dam, financed by USSR. South Africa: Police kill 67 black people in the Sharpeville massacre. U.S.: John F. Kennedy elected president (to 1963). American scientists develop lasers. First weather observation satellite launched.

1961 Tanzania becomes independent. Germany: Berlin Wall is built. USSR: Launches first manned spacecraft with Yuri Gagarin. Middle East: Organization of Petroleum Exporting Countries (OPEC) is formed. International crisis after the U.S. backs Bay of Pigs invasion (which fails) of communist Cuba.

1962 Tension between U.S. and USSR after discovery of Soviet missile bases on Cuba. South Vietnam: U.S. sets up military council to support government against Communists. Asia: India and China at war. U.S.: Riots when a Black student is admitted to University of Mississippi. Britain: Immigration is limited. Uganda becomes independent.

1963 France stops Britain joining EEC. U.S.: Freedom marches by civil rights' protesters. President Kennedy is assassinated. South Vietnam: Government overthrown; U.S. sends aid. Kenya, led by Jomo Kenyatta, and Malaysia, led by Tunku Abdul Rahman, become independent.

The assassination of John Kennedy touched the hearts of many people worldwide.

Wars in Asia

In 1950, many countries in the East had not yet recovered from Japanese invasions during World War II. People were exhausted, farms were neglected, and businesses were in ruins. They needed peace and stability, but many states were soon at war. These wars caused further damage, to people, cities, and the land. In some parts of the East, for example the Philippines, the political situation is still unstable.

Eastern countries fought for independence. They no longer wished to be colonies of some distant European power. The old colonial "masters" (France, Britain, and the Netherlands) wanted to hold on to these potentially rich lands. Fighting broke out in Vietnam (and its neighbors, Laos, Thailand, and Cambodia), Indonesia, Malaysia, Burma, and the Philippines.

These wars were often complicated by political differences between rival groups seeking independence. Some local

---

CAMBODIA

In 1970 the United States helped put Lon Nol in power in Cambodia. A rebel communist group, the Khmer Rouge, began fighting against the new rulers. By 1975 they had gained control. They enforced a brutal regime, resulting in the death of two million people. In 1978 Vietnamese forces invaded and overthrew the Khmer Rouge.

◀ American troops fought with the South Koreans against the North Koreans and Chinese during the Korean War (1950–1953). Helicopters were used intensively for the first time in this war (as they were later in Vietnam) to transport troops across difficult, mountainous territory in poor weather conditions.

▼ Fighting between rival political groups flared up in many parts of Asia between 1946 and 1988, following Japan's defeat in World War II and the collapse of European colonial power. Opponents were backed by superpowers: the U.S., USSR and, sometimes, China.

leaders wanted to set up a capitalist state after the colonial power had gone, others hoped to introduce a communist government. The situation became even more dangerous when the Soviet and U.S. superpowers joined in, offering money, weapons, or technical advice to these rival groups.

For example, in Korea, the country was divided into a communist north and a capitalist south. Troops from the north, helped by China, overran the south in 1950. So the Americans sent a large army to the south. In all over 3 million people were killed or made homeless before peace terms were agreed in 1953.

▶ During the Vietnam War (1964–1975), many parts of the country were devastated. The forests were sprayed with deadly chemicals to kill the undergrowth where rebels were hiding. Mines were planted as booby traps. Many civilians were killed and injured. Others were made homeless and fled as refugees to neighboring lands.

Common Markets

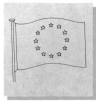

Throughout the world, neighboring states, or states with shared economic interests, have joined together to form powerful international associations. OPEC is probably the best known international trading association.

Some groups of states have also set up cooperative economic communities, known as "common markets." Within these markets, members buy and sell at favorable rates. They agree to protect one another from economic competition from outside. Often, strong political links develop between members.

Today's European Community (EC) is based on the former European Economic Community (EEC), set up in 1957 by the Treaty of Rome. Since then the original membership (France, Italy, West Germany, Netherlands, Belgium, and Luxembourg) has grown to include Britain, Ireland, Denmark, Greece, Spain,

OPEC

The Organization of Petroleum (oil) Exporting Countries was founded in 1961 to get the best price possible on world markets for its member states' oil. OPEC members include many Middle Eastern Arab states as well as Algeria, Indonesia, Nigeria, Ecuador, Gabon, and Venezuela. Between 1973 and 1974 OPEC quadrupled the price of crude oil. This led to a worldwide energy crisis.

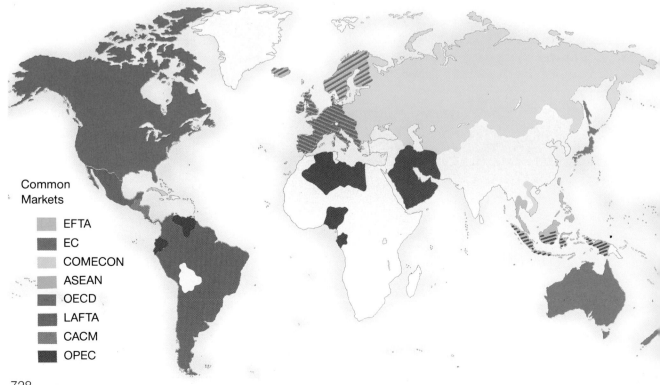

Common Markets

- EFTA
- EC
- COMECON
- ASEAN
- OECD
- LAFTA
- CACM
- OPEC

▲ *The EC headquarters building in Brussels, Belgium. The Community's administration is based there, and the parliament is in Strasbourg, France.*

and Portugal. There are plans for a single European currency, taxation, and law. There is already a European Parliament.

COMECON is a similar organization run by communist states. There are also "common markets" in Asia and Latin America. International groups, such as OECD, aim to protect weaker nations against powerful market forces, and to aid economic development.

◀ *International common markets and groupings of states with shared economic interests are found in all continents. In Europe the main common markets are the European Community (EC), the European Free Trade Association (EFTA), and the Soviet equivalent, the Council for Mutual Economic Assistance (COMECON), formed in 1949. The Central American Common Market (CACM) was set up in 1960, but was suspended in the 1980s. The Latin American Free Trade Association (LAFTA) was founded in 1961. The Association of Southeast Asian Nations (ASEAN) was set up in 1967 and includes non-communist countries. The Organization for Economic Cooperation and Development (OECD) started in Europe in 1948 and now includes the U.S.A. and Australia.*

1964 Malawi and Zambia become independent. Vietnam: War between North (backed by Communists) and South (backed by the U.S.). U.S.: Martin Luther King wins Nobel Peace Prize. Race riots in U.S. cities. British pop group The Beatles tour the U.S. Civil Rights Act becomes law. Britain: Exploration for North Sea oil and gas begins.

1965 Vietnam: U.S. troops arrive in South Vietnam. Rhodesia (Zimbabwe): Prime minister Ian Smith declares independence from Britain, and leads a white minority government which ignores Black Africans' rights. Britain: Designer Mary Quant launches the miniskirt.

1966 China: Cultural Revolution (to 1976). Vietnam: Australian troops fight alongside the Americans. Italy: Floods damage art treasures. U.S.: Anti-war demonstrations and race riots.

1967 Middle East: Six Day War between Israel and Arab states. Israel gains territory. Vietnam War: Efforts toward peace, but fighting starts again. Mass anti-war demonstrations in the U.S. and Europe. South Africa: first successful heart transplant operation performed. Europe: EEC becomes the European Community (EC). France again stops Britain joining. Caribbean: Anguilla becomes independent. Nigeria: Fighting begins in Biafra (to 1970); many die of starvation.

An offshore oil platform houses the drilling and extraction equipment and is used to store oil before it is pumped ashore.

1968 U.S.: Martin Luther King and Senator Robert Kennedy (presidential candidate) are assassinated. More race riots. Shirley Chisholm is first black woman to be elected to U.S. Congress. Vietnam War: Efforts toward peace, but fighting starts again. Czechoslovakia: Leader Alexander Dubček encourages free speech and independence from Soviets. USSR invades. Rhodesia: Talks between British prime minister Harold Wilson and Ian Smith of Rhodesia, fail. France: Student uprising in Paris.

The British- and French-built supersonic aircraft, Concorde, is capable of traveling at over twice the speed of sound.

1969 Northern Ireland: Fighting between Catholics and Protestants. Irish Republican Army (IRA) campaigns for an independent, united Ireland and the end of British rule. Czechoslovakia: USSR sets up new government which is loyal to Moscow. Nigeria: Red Cross leads international aid mission to relieve famine caused by the war between Biafrans, seeking independence, and the Nigerian government. Vietnam War: U.S. begins to withdraw troops from South Vietnam, but fighting (and anti-war protests) continues. U.S.: *Apollo 11* lands on the Moon and Neil Armstrong becomes the first man to walk on the Moon. Television pictures of his moonwalk are transmitted to Earth. Over 400,000 people attend a pop concert at Woodstock, New York State. Over 250,000 attend anti-war rally in Washington D.C. France: Supersonic aircraft *Concorde* makes first flight. President de Gaulle resigns. Georges Pompidou becomes president (to 1974).

New Nations

In the 1950s many military and political leaders in European colonies in Africa and the Far East campaigned for independence. They demanded the right to run their countries for themselves. Many of the independence movements were led by men of courage and vision. Often, they were imprisoned before gaining power.

Many countries used military force to win independence from colonial rule. During the 1950s and 1960s, many peoples in Africa and Southeast Asia were at war. European nations would not give up their power, and so freedom fighters, like the Mau Mau in Kenya, launched terrorist campaigns. In some states, as in Egypt in 1952–1953, independence came after the army took control. There were also civil wars, when minority tribal or religious groups within former European colonies sought to

◄ Countries that have gained independence since 1950 include many former European colonies in Africa and Southeast Asia, as well as territories in the Pacific, South America, the Middle East, and the Caribbean. In some cases, independence was won only after a bloody struggle. Life for new nations has been hard. Today, many of them are among the poorest in the world.

Countries that have gained independence since 1950

► Before Zimbabwe was born, there was conflict in the country (then Rhodesia). British soldiers, here talking to a commander in Robert Mugabe's army, formed part of a Commonwealth ceasefire-monitoring force.

▼ In 1961, protesters in the French colony of Algeria called for talks on independence between the French president, De Gaulle, and their leader Ferhat Abbas.

break free from majority control. In the civil war between Nigeria and the Biafra region (1967–1970) millions died.

Today most former colonies are independent. Some maintain ties, as do members of the British Commonwealth (*see* pages 714–715). Others have formed new alliances, such as the Organization for African Unity (OAU).

However, many former colonies are economically dependent. World trade is controlled by Europe, the United States, and Japan, and by multinational companies based largely in the West. It is hard for new nations not to fall into debt.

Wars in the Middle East

The area around the city of Jerusalem has been described for centuries as the traditional homeland of the Jewish people. However, Muslims and Christians have also lived there for hundreds of years. After World War II, over a million Jewish refugees from Europe settled in Palestine, although the area was occupied by Arab peoples. Following the formation of the state of Israel (*see* pages 710–711), fighting broke out with neighboring Arab countries and again in 1956, 1967, 1973, 1978, and 1982. Israel's occupation of the Gaza Strip and the West Bank were the cause of violent demonstrations which intensified in 1988, and the Palestine Liberation Organization (PLO) continues to fight for an Arab state in Palestine.

Between 1980 and 1988, Iran and Iraq were at war. Iraq (backed by the USSR and sometimes the U.S.) feared the power of the new Iranian government, set up by Ayatollah Khomeini after the shah had been overthrown.

▲ *Iranian protesters support the religious revolutionary leader, Ayatollah Khomeini (1900–1989), in 1979 during an anti-U.S. demonstration.*

▼ *The Six Day War took place between June 5 and 10, 1967. In a surprise attack, Israeli bombers destroyed Egyptian planes on the ground and followed this immediately with sending in troops to capture the Egyptian soldiers left in Sinai.*

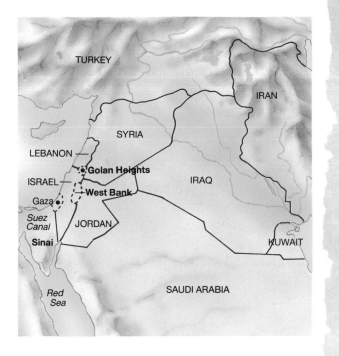

▲ *There have been conflicts between Israeli, Palestinian, and Arab peoples, particularly since 1948. Some areas of territory are still in dispute.*

Rivalries within the Arab world have been caused by the region's oil deposits. In 1990 Iraq invaded Kuwait to improve its sea access, and United Nations' forces fought to free Kuwait and safeguard oil supplies. Other tensions are caused by religious differences. There are two main forms of Islam, Sunni and Shiite. Sunni Muslims follow the "practice of the Prophet," Shiites follow the teachings of Muhammad's son-in-law, Ali.

THE SUEZ CRISIS

In July 1956, Egypt took over the Suez Canal which was owned by Britain and France. Because it felt threatened, Israel invaded Egyptian territory in Sinai, and Britain and France attacked the canal area. There was international disapproval and the United States and USSR both called for a ceasefire. After the withdrawal of Israeli, British, and French troops, a United Nations peace-keeping force arrived in Sinai. The UN troops were able to stop the Israelis and Arabs fighting for another ten years.

1970 Nigeria: Biafran war ends. Middle East: Truce between Israeli and Arab governments along borders of Suez Canal. Arab terrorists (protesting at U.S. support for Israel) hijack three passenger aircraft bound for U.S.. Egypt: Anwar Sadat becomes president (to 1981). Vietnam War: U.S. army invades Cambodia. U.S.: Student protest riots at 448 universities. Chile: Communist Salvador Allende becomes president. USSR: Soviet spacecraft lands on Venus.

1971 Vietnam War: Fighting spreads to Laos. U.S. bombs North Vietnam. Growing friendship between U.S. and China. Northern Ireland: Britain introduces internment (imprisonment without trial) following rioting. Bangladesh (formerly East Pakistan) becomes independent. Pakistan: War with India. USSR: Soviet spacecraft lands on Mars. Switzerland: Women get the vote.

1972 Germany: Arab terrorists kill Israeli athletes at Munich Olympics. Sri Lanka (formerly Ceylon) becomes independent. Northern Ireland: 13 Catholics are killed by British troops on "Bloody Sunday." Britain imposes direct rule. Vietnam War: Peace talks continue. Labor Party victories in elections in Australia and New Zealand lead to major changes. U.S.: Bobby Fischer becomes first American world chess champion. DDT insect-killer banned; start of government concern for environment.

Aircraft are frequently used to spray crops with plant food or insecticides (to prevent disease and attacks by insects) and herbicides (to kill weeds). Most of the sprays are bad for people if they breathe them in.

A map outlining the member countries of the European Community in 1973. Spain, Portugal, and Greece have since become members.

China and Japan

When Mao Zedong became chairman of the People's Republic of China in 1949, the civil war (*see* pages 672–673) had left the land poor and war-torn. The people were starving. Roads, railroads, schools, and hospitals could not meet the people's needs. Over the next 25 years, Mao transformed China. Collective farms grew basic foods, like rice, to feed the people. Industry produced more iron and steel. ''Barefoot doctors'' provided medical care to people in the countryside, and children learned to read and write. However, Mao's political opponents were executed, scholars were tortured, families were split up, and millions of people still died from famine. This was known as the

▲ The Thoughts of Chairman Mao *were studied by people all over China. They gave the required action for any situation. Here students chant from the book.*

JAPANESE TECHNOLOGY

Since the 1960s, Japanese manufacturers have pioneered the development of many new high-technology products. Japan manufactures a wide variety of objects including cars, computers, radios and televisions, and other electrical machines used in offices and factories throughout the world. Their factories are highly automated and robots are used on assembly lines to make production more efficient.

▲ In the spring of 1989 student demonstrators in Beijing and other cities in China called for freedom and democracy. The government sent in troops and tanks to crush the protests.

▼ When Mao came to power, many people in China were hungry. His government reorganized agriculture and created collective farms. Peasants and townspeople were put to work growing food.

Cultural Revolution. Mao was reacting because educated people criticized communism in the early 1960s. He was afraid that they would resist his extreme communist views. After Mao's death, the Chinese government became more open, and began to encourage contacts with the rest of the world. But the massacres that followed the student demonstrations in 1989 showed that full political freedom had not been achieved.

In Japan, government and business had to rebuild their economy after their defeat in World War II. They followed a different approach to China and planned a complete industrial redevelopment of their country, and rapid capitalist growth. Through the hard work and discipline of their people, they have been very successful. By 1990, Japan was one of the richest nations in the world.

In Hong Kong, one of the last British colonies, there was also fast economic growth. In 1984, Britain agreed to return Hong Kong to China in 1997 when the lease on the land runs out.

A Troubled World

Many parts of the world have been troubled by border disputes and civil wars. Families have been divided, economies have been weakened and torn apart by famine, disease, and death.

These conflicts have occurred because political boundaries between nations sometimes do not fit with traditional geographical, cultural, language, or religious frontiers. Groups like the Basques in Spain or the Shan peoples in Myanmar (Burma) can feel trapped within a larger state. Other peoples, such as the Eritreans and the Ethiopians in northeast Africa, who have different histories and traditions, have found themselves together in one "new nation" as a result of peace treaties or decisions made by former colonial powers.

▲ The Kurds' traditional homelands cross the borders of Turkey, Iran, and Iraq. When these countries are at war, suspicion falls on the Kurds. In 1990, many Kurds became refugees as they fled from Iraqi troops.

▼ After World War II, border disputes and wars between countries continued. Sometimes the wars, such as the Gulf War, involved other nations as well.

Many border disputes resulted from frontiers being drawn with no regard for the people in these regions. Civil wars have broken out, usually after years of discontent.

* Area of conflict
1. Cyprus
2. Lebanon
3. Israeli occupied territories (West Bank, Golan Heights Gaza Strip)
4. Yugoslavian Republics

Some groups of people use violence (terrorism) to gain publicity and win support for a political cause. They are often called freedom fighters by their supporters. Terrorists murder and kidnap people, set off bombs, and hijack aircraft. The reasons behind terrorism are not always the same. Some want to spread their own political beliefs, while others (nationalists or liberationists) want to establish a separate state for peoples who do not have a country of their own. For example, in the Middle East, terrorists have kidnapped people and carried out bombing campaigns to draw attention to the cause of the Palestinian people, who do not have a homeland. In Spain, a group known as ETA tries to pressurize the Spanish government into creating a separate state for the Basque people in the north of the country. But not all Palestinian or Basque people support the use of violence for political purposes.

▼ *A woman soldier in the Eritrean army. Since 1962 the Eritrean people have been fighting for independence from Ethiopia.*

1976 North and South Vietnam are united under communist rule. Cambodia: Pol Pot comes to power; he and his followers massacre many civilians. Thailand: Military coup. Earthquakes in China, the Philippines, Bali, Turkey, and Guatemala kill 780,000 people. China: Chairman Mao Zedong dies. South Africa: Riots against apartheid in Soweto and other Black townships. Nicaragua: Civil war (to 1979). Lebanon: Fighting among Syrians, Palestinians, Lebanese Christians, and Muslims. Canada: French-Canadians campaign for independent Quebec state. Angola: Outbreak of civil war. U.S.: First fears expressed by U.S. scientists about damage to ozone layer. Episcopal Church approves ordination of women to priesthood. France: The Pompidou Center is built in Paris.

1977 Czechoslovakia: New protests against Soviet control. USSR: Civil rights' protesters arrested. Ethiopia: Civil war. Zaire: Katanga rebels from Angola invade, but are defeated (and in 1978). U.S.: Tests neutron bomb. Rhodesia (now Zimbabwe): White rebels agree to Black majority rule.

1978 Nicaragua: Sandinista rebels fight against U.S.-backed government. Italy: Former prime minister, Aldo Moro, is killed by Red Brigades' terrorists (left-wing). Britain: First test-tube baby is born. Vietnam invades Cambodia.

The Pompidou Center was designed by Piano and Rogers to have its pipes and ducts on the outside, to create more interior space.

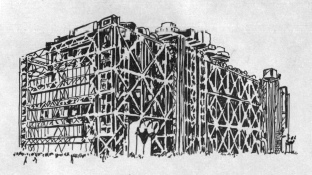

1979 Israel and Egypt sign peace treaty. Central America: Sandinistas win civil war in Nicaragua. Rebellion in El Salvador. Iran: Shah is replaced by Islamic republican government led by Ayatollah Khomeini. Iranian students seize American embassy and take hostages. Afghanistan: Soviet invasion. Fighting between Vietnam and China. Margaret Thatcher becomes first woman prime minister of Britain.

1980 Turkey: Military coup. Middle East: War between Iran and Iraq (to 1988). Poland: Solidarity, the independent trade union led by Lech Walesa, is formed. Yugoslavia: Marshal Tito, the president, dies. Communist government faces demands for regional independence. U.S.: Illnesses caused by AIDS virus first recognized. Beginning of "silicon revolution;" computers widely used in business and industry.

1981 Poland: Government crackdown on all trade unions. Egypt: President Sadat assassinated. Northern Ireland: IRA hunger strikes. Greece joins EC. U.S.: First space shuttle flight. France: François Mitterand becomes president.

1982 Argentina occupies Falkland Islands. Britain sends troops to force Argentinians to leave. West Germany: Helmut Kohl becomes chancellor. Spain joins NATO.

1983 Caribbean: U.S. invades Grenada to stop army taking control. Argentina: New democratic leadership elected.

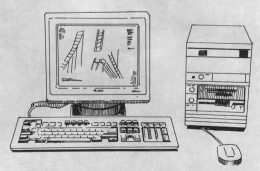

The personal computer has revolutionized the end of the 20th century and greatly affected the way we live our lives today.

Change in Eastern Europe

Mikhail Gorbachev became leader of the USSR in 1985. His appointment led to enormous changes as he tried to strengthen the Soviet economy and to reduce corruption. He dismissed inefficient local officials, reformed the way elections were carried out, encouraged private enterprise in agriculture, and introduced policies of "perestroika" (economic reform) and "glasnost" (openness). He called for cuts in army spending and for friendship between the Warsaw Pact countries and the West.

Gorbachev's reforms were welcomed by most of the Soviet people as they had more freedom, but this new freedom uncovered problems. The republics of Estonia, Latvia, and Lithuania, and Georgia demanded freedom from Communist Party control. In Armenia

SOLIDARITY

Solidarity was formed in 1980 in Poland, to campaign for workers' rights, better conditions, and freedom from communist control. At first it was banned and its leader, Lech Walesa, arrested. The people continued to press for reforms and Solidarity was finally recognized in 1989.

and Azerbaijan there were violent clashes between Christians and Muslims.

Powerful Soviet politicians feared that Gorbachev's reforms would lead to the collapse of the USSR and tried to take over the government in 1991. They failed and at the end of the year the old USSR was abolished and replaced by an alliance of independent states. Gorbachev resigned and Boris Yeltsin became president of Russia.

Similar upheavals were taking place in other parts of Europe. After almost 30 years, the Berlin Wall was demolished and East and West Germany were reunited in 1990. The reunification caused problems for the strong West German economy as efforts were made to modernize equipment and industry throughout eastern Germany.

In the previously communist countries of Hungary, Poland, Czechoslovakia, Romania, and Bulgaria, new liberal groups came to power and struggled to adapt to a capitalist economy. Yugoslavia also struggled with a bitter civil war as three provinces, Bosnia, Croatia, and Slovenia fought for independence from a Yugoslav state dominated by Serbia.

▲ Crowds lining outside a McDonald's restaurant in Moscow in 1989. It was one of the first Western enterprises to open in the USSR, which had previously been very against Western influences.

▼ The Berlin Wall was built in 1961 to isolate the western part of the city from the east. Anyone trying to cross it from the east was killed. In 1989 Berliners celebrated as the wall came down and the guards left.

The Scientific Revolution

The second half of the 20th century has been a period of rapid development in science and technology. Scientists and business people have been able to develop the discoveries made earlier in the century, and put them to practical use. One of the most important inventions was the silicon chip, a tiny component which could be cheaply mass-produced. It replaced old, bulky, and fragile pieces of equipment, and enabled machines such as smaller calculators and computers to be built. Machines like these, along with photocopiers and faxes, meant that office workers could handle vast amounts of information more quickly than before. They could also communicate rapidly with other offices around the world.

Lasers were used in surgery to burn away diseased tissue. They also had many military uses. British and American scientists discovered the structure of DNA, the basic building blocks from which living cells are made. This knowledge led eventually to the

---

SILICON WAFERS

Silicon wafers or chips are "printed" with tiny electric circuits that enable computers to process and store information. The first silicon chip microprocessor was developed in 1971 in the U.S.A. Since then new industries have grown up, using silicon-chip based technology. These include control systems for factories, aircraft, and cars.

SCIENTIFIC ACHIEVEMENTS

1950 First color television program is broadcast in the United States.

1952 Acrilan, a synthetic fiber used for making cloth, is discovered.

1955 The first anti-polio vaccine is made available after being declared safe and effective.

1959 First photocopier is introduced.

1962 Launch of the communications satellite, *Telstar*. It is used to transmit the first trans-Atlantic television pictures.

1967 First tidal power station opens across the Rance river estuary in France.

1968 Regular hovercraft service starts across the English Channel.

1978 Solar-powered calculators are first sold in the U.S.

1979 Personal computers are launched.

1982 Compact disc players are first introduced.

1983 HIV retrovirus, from which AIDS can result, first identified in France and U.S.

1987 First criminal convicted as a result of genetic fingerprinting.

▶ *The green revolution aims to help farmers grow more food using better seeds and fertilizers. Higher-yielding crops are being produced but the cost of fertilizer presents a problem in some countries.*

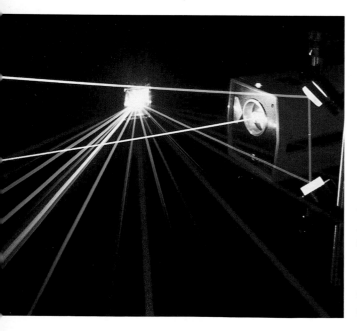

◀ *Since lasers were invented in 1960 they have been used for a wide range of purposes including eye surgery, construction work, and light shows.*

▲ Concorde *went into service in 1976. It was the world's first supersonic passenger aircraft, and was built by a team of French and English engineers.*

production of new drugs by genetic engineering which helped cure serious diseases. It also raised the possibility of new or improved strains of plants and animals being created in laboratories.

In some countries, new technology made life easier. Many people owned washing machines, refrigerators, and freezers. Home entertainment was transformed by televisions, VCRs, music tapes, and compact discs.

1984 India: President Indira Gandhi is assassinated by Sikh militants. Famine in Ethiopia. Britain agrees to return Hong Kong to China in 1997.

1985 USSR: President Chernenko, succeeded by Mikhail Gorbachev (to 1991) who introduces major reforms. South Africa: Apartheid policies slowly being relaxed. Marriages between black and white people become legal. South Pacific Forum draws up Nuclear Free Zone Treaty. New Zealand bans nuclear weapons; France continues nuclear tests. Pop singer Bob Geldof organizes Live Aid charity pop concerts in Britain and United States to raise money for famine victims in Ethiopia; they are seen by the largest-ever TV audience. World population now 4.5 billion; scientists predict that it will reach 6–9 billion by the year 2000.

1986 Libya: U.S. bombs Tripoli and Benghazi in retaliation for Libyan support for anti-American terrorist campaigns. Europe: Spain and Portugal join the EC. South Africa: Widespread fighting in Black townships by civil rights' protesters. Rival Black political groups (ANC and Inkatha) also clash. USSR: Accident at Chernobyl nuclear reactor causes massive leak of radioactive particles. U.S.: Space shuttle *Challenger* explodes after takeoff, killing the crew of seven. Airplane *Voyager* becomes first to circumnavigate the globe without refueling. USSR: *Mir* space station is launched.

The logo used to promote the Live Aid concerts that raised money for famine victims.

741

1987 U.S. and USSR agree to ban medium-range nuclear weapons. Middle East: Violent rioting by Palestinians and attacks in return by Israeli troops cause widespread international concern. European Community (EC): Members meet to plan eventual European union. New rules (to be introduced in 1992) aim to achieve unified laws, taxes, welfare benefits, and currency, also a European army and police force. Bangladesh: Monsoon makes 24 million people homeless. Scientists confirm existence of a hole in the ozone layer above Antarctica.

1988 End of Iran-Iraq War. USSR: New constitution (system of government) introduced allowing greater freedom of speech and less Communist Party control. Pakistan: Benazir Bhutto becomes prime minister (to 1990) and the first woman to govern an Islamic republic. Israel occupies Gaza Strip.

1989 USSR: Demonstrations in Estonia by local Communist Party and nationalist groups wanting freedom from Soviet control. Demands for independence in Lithuania. Afghanistan: Soviet president Gorbachev decides to withdraw Soviet troops from Afghanistan. Romania: Dictator Ceaucescu is overthrown. China: Student demonstrations in Beijing calling for greater freedom and democracy are crushed by government troops. Namibia: First free elections are held. Muslims call for death of British author Salman Rushdie after publication of his novel *The Satanic Verses*. Iran: Ayatollah Khomeini dies.

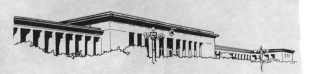

Chinese Government buildings beside Tiananmen Square, Beijing, where many people lost their lives when government troops suppressed a student demonstration.

Social Change

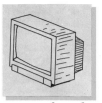

During the late l960s, many young people took part in protest movements. They were calling for a social revolution based on peace, freedom, and understanding. Few of their aims were achieved. However, there were other, slower changes taking place in society.

The number of people in the world was growing fast and there was an increasing awareness of the problems of feeding them all. International bodies such as the United Nations gave aid, along with charities in wealthy countries but the gap between rich and poor got wider.

In rich countries, the power of the press, television, and advertising grew rapidly. As a result a consumer society

▼ *Signs like this were widespread in South Africa while the government encouraged the policy of apartheid (separation of black and white people). It was finally abolished in 1990.*

▶ *One of the largest fund-raising pop concerts was organized by Bob Geldof in 1985. He was appalled by reports of the 1984 famine in Ethiopia, and planned the Live Aid concert to raise money to send food and expert help. It was broadcast live in many countries.*

developed, concerned with quality of life, fashion, and style. Education led to improved opportunities for many young people, but there was still inequality between and within different racial groups, in spite of the activities of civil rights campaigners. With the greater ability to travel and greater distances between people, communities changed as did families as divorce and single-parent families became more common.

The position of women is changing and improving as their equal social and legal rights are clarified and reinforced.

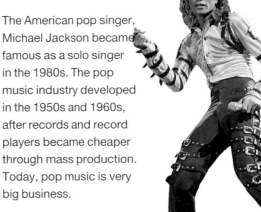

POP CULTURE

The American pop singer, Michael Jackson became famous as a solo singer in the 1980s. The pop music industry developed in the 1950s and 1960s, after records and record players became cheaper through mass production. Today, pop music is very big business.

EDUCATION

In many countries, people were better educated than before. School graduation ages were raised and higher education was available for more students. Education and qualifications were seen as essential, as a pathway to a good job. In other countries the lack of teachers and facilities meant that children received only a basic education. Opportunities for adult education increased.

WOMEN

The 1960s and 1970s saw the rise of the women's movement. Women demanded equal opportunities and the same pay as men and an end to discrimination based on sexism. Women took traditionally male jobs and proved they could succeed. Women also campaigned for recognition of the important job they did as homemakers and child-carers.

▲ *A Chinese government poster, encouraging couples to have only one child. For several years, it has been illegal for Chinese people to have more children. Other governments tried to restrict population growth but only some have been successful.*

1990 Gulf War: Iraq invades Kuwait. UN forces sent to the area. Eastern Europe: Political unrest continues. Soviet troops intervene in ethnic violence between Armenia and Azerbaijan. East and West Germany are reunited as one nation. South Africa: Veteran anti-apartheid campaigner Nelson Mandela is released from prison; he continues his leadership of African National Congress (ANC). Apartheid abolished. Britain: Margaret Thatcher resigns after 11 years in power.

1991 UN forces Iraq to withdraw from Kuwait. USSR: Hardline Communists attempt a coup, but meet resistance led by Russian leader Boris Yeltsin. Mikhail Gorbachev resigns as leader, the USSR is officially dissolved. Yugoslavia: Civil war breaks out as individual states fight about independence (Slovenia and Croatia) and federation. Lebanon: Remaining U.S. and British hostages held by Muslim groups are released.

1992 European Community: Single European Act brings unity closer, although states disagree on some issues. Africa: Famine threat. Fears that ozone layer over Europe is thinning rapidly. Brazil: UN Earth summit is held to discuss world environmental concerns. Czechoslovakia: Czechs and Slovaks agree to form separate governments.

1993 Yugoslavia: Civil war intensifies as Serbia fights to maintain federation. US: Bill Clinton is inaugurated as president.

Nelson Mandela was released from prison after 27 years, having been convicted of sabotage and conspiracy.

Environmental Concerns

For centuries, people believed that nature should be tamed and controlled. In the latter half of the 20th century, people realized the Earth was in danger, threatened with pollution and over-exploitation as a result of ignorance and greed. At first, only a few naturalists, like Rachel Carson, whose book *Silent Spring* caused a sensation when it was published in the 1950s, dared to speak up. Then pressure groups, such as Greenpeace, also began to campaign. By the 1980s, some governments passed laws to protect the environment, but some scientists believed that these attempts to protect our planet might be too little and too late.

Change was slow to take effect because at first people did not believe that the Earth was really in danger. New information was collected by scientists which proved that the threat was real. Clean (non-polluting) products started to appear but they proved expensive to buy and less profitable to produce. It took environmental disasters such as accidents at nuclear reactors in the U.S. and the

▲ *In the Mato Grosso in Brazil, huge areas of rain forest are being destroyed so that local farmers can graze cattle on the land, and to sell the valuable timber.*

USSR, explosions at chemical plants in Italy and India, and oil spillages at sea to show people that new technology could be deadly. Then public opinion forced governments to take action and try to halt pollution. The discovery of holes in the ozone layer around the Earth, and possible worldwide climatic change have encouraged environmental concern.

In environmental matters we have, unfortunately, little to learn from the past, but there is much in history that we must continue to remember in order to avoid disaster. We must also be ruthless in remembering ideas and practices that have been important in the past but which would be fatal for all our futures.

▲ Seas around the world have been polluted because they are used to dump household and industrial waste. It is either discharged directly into the sea or dumped from boats.

▶ Oil spills are caused either by accidents involving oil tankers, or as waste-oil is discharged into the sea when ships clean out their tanks. The oil floats on the sea's surface, forming a slow-moving slick covering fish, birds, and sea creatures. Most of them die.

▼ After the explosion at the nuclear power station at Chernobyl, USSR, in 1986, houses nearby were hosed down to get rid of the contamination. The people were moved away but many still suffer from the after-effects.

ACID RAIN

In northern Europe, the U.S., and Canada, waste gases from power stations burning oil and coal drift over lakes and forests and mix with rain to produce a weak acid. Scientists think that this acid rain has damaged and killed millions of trees, polluted waterways, and killed fish.

RECYCLING

Many of the resources on the Earth are non-renewable (cannot be recreated). These include most of our energy sources such as coal and oil, and the raw materials that go to make goods. It is now economic to recycle (use again) many things we use daily, such as paper, cans, and glass.

Ready Reference

ANCIENT EGYPTIAN DYNASTIES

Period	Dynasty	Dates (B.C.)	Principal pharaohs
Early Dynastic	1–3	c. 2920–2575	Menes (Aha)
			Zoser (Djoser)
Old Kingdom	4–7/8	c. 2575–2134	Cheops (Khufu)
First Intermediate Period	9–11	c. 2134–2040	
Middle Kingdom	11–14	c. 2040–1532	Mentuhotep II
Second Intermediate Period	15–17	1640–1532	Hyksos kings in north Kamose reunites Egypt
New Kingdom	18–20	1550–1070	Amenhotep I–III (Amenophis)
			Thutmosis I–IV
			Queen Hatshepsut
			Akhenaten (Amenhotep IV)
			Tutankhamun
			Rameses I–XI
Third Intermediate Period	21–25	1070–712	Sheshonq I
			Rule of Nubians
Late Period	25–31	712–332	Psammetichus I
			Rule of Persians
			Nectanebo II
			Conquest of Alexander the Great

CHINESE DYNASTIES

Dynasty	Date	Details
Hsia	c. 2205–1500 B.C.	
Shang	1500–1122	
Zhou	1122–256	
Qin	221–207	Shi Huangdi, first emperor of unified China
Early Han	202 B.C.–A.D. 9	Emperor Wu-ti also rules Korea and north Vietnam
Hsin	5–23	Usurpation of Wang Mang
Later Han	25–220	
The Three Kingdoms	220–265	China breaks into three kingdoms – the Wei, Shu, and Wu
Western Chin	265–317	
Eastern Chin	317–420	
Southern dynasties	420–589	
Sui	581–618	China reunified
Tang	618–907	Golden age of culture; includes reign of Emperor T'ai Tsung the Great
The five dynasties and ten kingdoms	907–960	Period of disunity
Liao	947–1125	Part of northern China ruled by Khitan Mongols
Song	960–1279	Dynasty rules parts of China only
Northern Song	960–1126	
Western Hsia	990–1227	
Chin	1115–1234	
Southern Song	1127–1279	
Yuan (Mongol)	1279–1368	All China ruled by the Mongols led by Kublai Khan
Ming	1368–1644	Reestablishment of a native Chinese dynasty
Qing (Manchu)	1644–1911	
Republic of China	1911–1949	Government set up under Sun Yat-sen, followed by disunity and the warlord era
People's Republic	1949–	Mao Zedong is first chairman of Communist Party

ROMAN RULERS

Kings of Rome

Romulus	753–716 B.C.	Tarquinius Priscus	616–579
Numa Pompilius	716–673	Servius Tullius	579–534
Tullus Hostilius	673–640	Tarquinius Superbus	534–509
Ancus Martius	640–616		

The Republic of Rome

Dictatorship of Sulla	82–78	Dictatorship of Julius Caesar	45–44
First Triumvirate (Julius Caesar, Pompey, and Crassus)	60–53	Second Triumvirate (Octavian, Mark Anthony and Marcus Lepidus)	43–27
Dictatorship of Pompey	52–47		

Emperors of the Roman Empire

Augustus (previously Octavian)	27 B.C.–A.D. 14	Gallus and Hostilianus (Volusianus)	251–253
Tiberius I	AD 14–37	Aemilianus	253
Caligula (Gaius Caesar)	37–41	Valerian and Gallienus	253–260
Claudius I	41–54	Gallienus	260–268
Nero	54–68	Claudius II (Gothicus)	268–270
Galba	68–69	Quintillus	270
Otho	69	Aurelianus	270–275
Vitellius	69	Tacitus	275–276
Vespasian	69–79	Florianus	276
Titus	79–81	Probus	276–282
Domitian	81–96	Carus	282–283
Nerva	96–98	Carinus and Numerianus	283–284
Trajan	98–117	Diocletian (divides empire)	284–305
Hadrian	117–138	Maximian (jointly)	286–305
Antoninus Pius	138–161	Constantius I	305–306
Marcus Aurelius	161–180	Severus	306–307
Lucius Verus (jointly)	161–169	Licinius (jointly)	307–323
Commodus	180–192	Constantine I (reunites empire)	308–337
Pertinax	193	Constantine II (jointly)	337–340
Didius Julianus	193	Constans (jointly)	337–350
Septimus Severus	193–211	Constantius II (jointly)	337–361
Caracalla	211–217	Magnentius (jointly)	350–353
Geta (jointly)	211–212	Julian (the Apostate)	361–363
Macrinus	217–218	Jovianus	363–364
Elagabulus (Heliogabalus)	218–222	Valentinian I (rules West)	364–375
Alexander Severus	222–235	Valens (rules East)	364–378
Maximinius I (the Thracian)	235–238	Gratian (rules West)	375–383
Gordian I	238	Magnus Maximus (usurper in West)	383–388
Gordian II	238	Valentinian II (rules West)	375–392
Balbinus and Pupienus Maximus	238	Eugenius (usurper in West)	392–394
Gordian III	238–244	Theodosius I (the Great) (rules East, then unites East and West)	378–395
Philip (the Arab)	244–249		
Decius	249–251		

Emperors of the Eastern Roman Empire

Arcadius	395–408	Leo II	474
Theodosius II	408–450	Zeno	474–491
Marcian	450–457	Anastasius	491–518
Leo I	457–474		

Emperors of the Western Roman Empire

Honorius	395–423	Majorian	457–461
Maximus	410–411	Severus III	461–465
Constantius III	421	Anthemius	467–472
John	423–425	Olybrius	472
Valentinian III	425–455	Glycerius	473
Petronius Maximus	455	Julius Nepos	473–480
Avitus	455–456	Romulus Augustus	475–476

ARGENTINA

Presidents (since 1854)

Justo José Urquiza	1854–1860	Augustín P. Justo	1932–1938
Santiago Derqui	1860–1862	Roberto M. Ortiz	1938–1942
Bartolomé Mitre	1862–1868	Ramón S. Castillo	1942–1943
Domingo Faustino Sarmiento	1868–1874	Pedro Ramirez	1943–1944
Nicolás Avellaneda	1874–1880	Edelmiro J. Farrell	1944–1946
Julio Argentino Roca	1880–1886	Juan Domingo Perón	1946–1955
Miguel Juárez Celmán	1886–1890	Pedro Eugenion Aramburu (provisional)	1955–1958
Carlos Pellegrini	1890–1892	Arturo Frondizi	1958–1962
Luis Sáenz Peña	1892–1895	José María Guido	1962–1963
José Evaristo Uriburu	1895–1898	Arturo Umberto Illia	1963–1966
Julio Argentino Roca	1898–1904	Juan Carlos Onganía	1966–1970
Manuel Quintana	1904–1906	Roberto Marcelo Levingston	1970–1971
José Figueroa Alcorta	1906–1910	Alejandro Agustin Lanusse	1971–1973
Roque Sáenz Peña	1910–1914	Héctor J. Cámpora	1973
Victorino de la Plaza	1914–1916	Juan Domingo Perón	1973–1974
Hipólito Irigoyen	1916–1922	Isabel Perón	1974–1976
Marcelo Torcuato de Alvear	1922–1928	Military Junta	1976–1983
Hipólito Irigoyen	1928–1930	Raúl Alfonsín	1983–1989
José Francisco Uriburu (provisional)	1930–1932	Carlos Menem	1989–

BRAZIL

Presidents

Manuel Deodoro da Fonesca	1889–1891	José Linhares (provisional)	1945–1946
Floriano Peixoto	1891–1894	Enrico Gaspar Dutra	1946–1951
Prudente José de Moraes Barros	1894–1898	Getúlio Dornelles Vargas	1951–1954
Manuel Ferraz de Campos Salles	1898–1902	João Café Filho	1954–1955
Francisco de Paula Rodrigues Alves	1902–1906	Nereú Ramos (acting)	1955–1956
Affonso Augusto Moreira Penna	1906–1909	Jusceline Kubitschek de Oliveira	1956–1961
Nilo Peçanha	1909–1910	Jânio Quadros	1961
Hermes da Fonseca	1910–1914	João Belchior Marques Goulart	1961–1964
Wenceslau Braz Pereira Gomes	1914–1918	Humberto Castelo Branco	1964–1967
Francisco de Paula Rodrigues Alves	1918–1919	Arthur Costa e Silva	1967–1969
Delfim Moreira (acting)	1918–1919	Emilio Garrastazú Médici	1969–1974
Epitacio da Silva Pessôa	1919–1922	Ernesto Geisel	1974–1979
Arthur da Silva Bernardes	1922–1926	João Baptista Figueiredo	1979–1985
Washington Luiz Pereira de Souza (deposed)	1926–1930	José Sarney	1985–1990
		Fernando Collor de Mello	1990–1992
Getulio Dornelles Vargus	1930–1945	Itamar Franco	1992–

MEXICO

Presidents (since 1824)

Guadalupe Victoria	1824–1829	José Joaquin Herrera	1844–1845
Vicente Guerrero	1829	Mariano Paredes y Arrillaga	1846
José María de Bocanegra (acting)	1829	Nicolás Bravo	1846
Anastasio Bustamante	1829–1832	José Mariano Salas (acting)	1846
Melchor Múzquiz (acting)	1832	[War with the United States, 1846–1848]	
Manuel Gómez Pedraza	1832–1833	Valentin Gómez Farias (acting)	1846–1847
Antonio López de Santa Anna	1833–1835	Antonio López de Santa Anna	1847
Miguel Barragán	1835–1836	Pedro María Anaya	1847
José Justo Corro	1836–1837	Antonio López de Santa Anna	1847
Anastasio Bustamente*	1837–1841	Manuel de la Peña y Peña (provisional)	1847
Javier Echeverria (acting)	1841	Pedro María Anaya (acting)	1847–1848
Antonio López de Santa Anna	1841–1842	Manuel de la Peña y Peña	1848
Nicolás Bravo	1842–1843	José Joaquin Herrera	1848–1851
Antonio López de Santa Anna (provisional)	1843	Mariano Arista	1851–1853
		Juan Bautista Ceballos (acting)	1853
Valentín Canalizo	1843–1844	Manuel M. Lombardine (acting)	1853
Antonio López de Santa Anna	1844	Antonio López de Santa Anna (dictator)	1853–1855
José Joaquin Herrera (acting)	1844	Martin Carrera (acting)	1855
Valentín Canalizo (acting)	1844	Juan Alvarez (acting)	1855

Ignacio Comonfort	1855–1857	Francisco Lagos Cházaro (provisional)	1915
Benito Juárez (provisional)	1857–1861	Venustiano Carranza (provisional)	1915–1917
Benito Juárez	1861–	Venustiano Carranza	1917–1920
[Period of French intervention, 1861–1867.		Adolfo de la Huerta (provisional)	
Austrian Archduke Maximilian crowned Emperor,		Alvaro Obregón	1920–1924
June 12, 1864; executed June 19, 1867]		Plutarco Elías Calles	1924–1928
Sebastian Lerdo de Tejada	1872–	Emilio Portes Gil (provisional)	1928–1930
Porfirio Díaz (provisional)		Pascual Ortiz Rubio	1930–1932
Juan N. Méndez (acting)	1876–	Abelardo L. Rodriquez (provisional)	1932–1934
Porfirio Díaz (provisional)		Lázaro Cárdenas	1934–1940
Porfirio Díaz	1877–1880	Manuel Avila Camacho	1940–1946
Manuel González	1880–1884	Miguel Alemán Valdés	1946–1952
Porfirio Díaz	1884–	Adolfo Ruiz Cortines	1952–1958
Francisco León de la Barra (provisional)		Adolfo López Mateos	1958–1964
Francisco Indalecio Madero	1911–1913	Gustavo Díaz Ordaz	1964–1970
Victoriano Huerta (provisional)	1913–1914	Luis Echeverría Alvarez	1970–1976
Francisco Carbajal (provisional)	1914	José López Portillo	1976–1982
Venustiano Carranza ("first chief")	1914	Miguel de la Madrid Huertad	1982–1988
Eulalio Martin Gutiérrez (provisional)	1914–1915	Carlos Salinas de Gortari	1988–
Roque Gonzalez Garza	1915		

*From March 18 to July 10, 1839, Santa Anna was in control; from July 10 to 17, 1839, Nicolas Bravo was acting president.

PERU

Presidents (since 1821)

José de San Martín	1821–1822	Manuel Candamo	1903–1904
José de la Riva Aguero	1823	Serapio Calderón (acting)	May–Sept. 1904
Simón Bolívar (dictator)	1824–1827	José Pardo y Barreda	1904–1908
José de Lamar	1827–1829	Augusto Bernardino Leguía y Salcedo	1908–1912
Agustin Gamarra	1829–1833	Guillermo Enrique Billinghurst	1912–1914
Luis José Orbegosa	1833–1835	Oscar Raimundo Benavides	1915
Felipe Santiago Salaverry	1835–1836	(provisional)	
Andrés Santa Cruz	1836–1839	José Pardo y Barreda	1915–1919
Agustin Gamarra	1839–1841	Augusto Bernardino Leguía y Salcedo	1919–1930
Manuel Menéndez* (acting)	1841–1845	Manuel Ponce (provisional)	1930
Ramón Castilla	1845–1851	Luis M. Sánchez Cerro (provisional)	1930–1931
José Rufino Echenique	1851–1855	Ricardo Leoncio Elías (provisional)	1931
Ramón Castilla	1855–1862	Gustavo Jiménez (provisional)	1931
Miguel San Román	1862–1863	David Samánez Ocampo (provisional)	1931
Juan Antonio Pezet	1863–1865	Luis M. Sánchez Cerro	1931–1933
Mariano Ignacio Prado (dictator)	1865–1868	Oscar Raimundo Benavides	1833–1939
José Balta	1868–1872	Manuel Prado Ugarteche	1939–1945
Manuel Pardo	1872–1876	José Luis Bustamante Rivero	1945–1948
Mariano Ignacio Prado	1876–1879	Manuel Odría (provisional)	1948–1950
Nicolás de Piérola	1879–1881	Zenón Noriega	1950
Francisco García Calderón	1881	Manuel Odría	1950–1956
Lizardo Montero	1881–1883	Manuel Prado y Ugarteche	1956–1962
Miguel Iglesias	1883–1886	Ricardo Pérez Godoy (provisional)	1962
Andrés Avelino Cáceres	1886–1890	Fernando Belaúnde Terry	1963–1968
Remigio Morales Bermúdez	1890–1894	Military rule	1968–1980
Justíniano Borgoño	1894	Fernando Belaúnde Terry	1980 1985
Andrés Avelino Cáceres	1894–1895	Alan Garcia Pérez	1985–1990
Nicolás de Piérola	1895–1899	Alberto Fujimori	1990–
Eduardo Lopez de Romaña	1899–1903		

*The period 1841–1844 was one of civil war and confusion. Juan Crisóstomo Terrico and Manuel Vivanco were each for a short time in power.

RULERS OF ENGLAND

Saxons

Egbert	827–839	Ethelbert	860–865
Ethelwulf	839–858	Ethelred I	865–871
Ethelbald	858–860	Alfred the Great	871–899

Edward the Elder	899–924	Edgar	959–975
Athelstan	924–939	Edward the Martyr	975–978
Edmund	939–946	Ethelred II, the Unready	978–1016
Edred	946–955	Edmund Ironside	
Edwy	955–959		

Danes

Canute	1016–1035	Harthacanute	1040–1042
Harold I Harefoot	1035–1040		

Saxons

Edward the Confessor	1042–1066	Harold II	1066

House of Normandy

William I, the Conqueror	1066–1087	Henry I	1100–1135
William II	1087–1100	Stephen	1135–1154

House of Plantagenet

Henry II	1154–1189	Edward I	1272–1307
Richard I, the Lionheart	1189–1199	Edward II	1307–1327
John	1199–1216	Edward III	1327–1377
Henry III	1216–1272	Richard II	1377–1399

House of Lancaster

Henry IV	1399–1413	Henry VI	1422–1461
Henry V	1413–1422		

House of York

Edward IV	1461–1483	Richard III	1483–1485
Edward V	1483		

House of Tudor

Henry VII	1485–1509	Mary I	1553–1558
Henry VIII	1509–1547	Elizabeth I	1558–1603
Edward VI	1547–1553		

RULERS OF SCOTLAND

Malcolm II	1005–1034	Alexander II	1214–1249
Duncan I	1034–1040	Alexander III	1249–1286
Macbeth (usurper)	1040–1057	Margaret of Norway	1286–1290
Malcolm III (Cranmore)	1057–1093		
Donald Bane	1093–1094	(Interregnum	1290–1292)
Duncan II	1094		
Donald Bane (restored)	1094–1097	John Balliol	1292–1296
Edgar	1097–1107		
Alexander I	1107–1124	(Interregnum	1296–1306)
David I	1124–1153		
Malcolm IV	1153–1165	Robert I, the Bruce	1306–1329
William the Lion	1165–1214	David II	1329–1371

House of Stuart

Robert II	1371–1390	James IV	1488–1513
Robert III	1390–1406	James V	1513–1542
James I	1406–1437	Mary, Queen of Scots	1542–1567
James II	1437–1460	James VI (I of Great Britain)	1567–1625
James III	1460–1488		

RULERS OF ENGLAND AND SCOTLAND

House of Stuart

James I	1603–1625	Charles I	1625–1649

Commonwealth	**1649–1653;**		
Protectorate	**1653–1660**		
Oliver Cromwell	1649–1658		
Richard Cromwell	1658–1659		

House of Stuart

Charles II	1660–1685	William III (jointly)	1689–1702
James II	1685–1688	Anne	1702–1714
Mary II (jointly)	1689–1694		

RULERS OF GREAT BRITAIN

House of Hanover

George I	1714–1727	George IV	1820–1830
George II	1727–1760	William IV	1830–1837
George III	1760–1820	Victoria	1837–1901

House of Saxe-Coburg

Edward VII	1901–1910

House of Windsor

George V	1910–1936	George VI	1936–1952
Edward VIII	1936	Elizabeth II	1952–

PRIME MINISTERS OF GREAT BRITAIN

	In office	Party
Sir Robert Walpole	1721–1742	Whig
Earl of Wilmington	1742–1743	Whig
Henry Pelham	1743–1754	Whig
Duke of Newcastle	1754–1756	Whig
Duke of Devonshire	1756–1757	Whig
Duke of Newcastle	1757–1762	Whig
Earl of Bute	1762–1763	Tory
George Grenville	1763–1765	Whig
Marquess of Rockingham	1765–1766	Whig
William Pitt the Elder (Earl of Chatham)	1766–1768	Whig
Duke of Grafton	1767–1770	Whig
Lord North	1770–1782	Tory
Marquess of Rockingham	1782	Whig
Earl of Shelburne	1782–1783	Whig
Duke of Portland	1783	Coalition
William Pitt the Younger	1783–1801	Tory
Henry Addington	1801–1804	Tory
William Pitt the Younger	1804–1806	Tory
Lord Grenville	1806–1807	Whig
Duke of Portland	1807–1809	Tory
Spencer Perceval	1809–1812	Tory
Earl of Liverpool	1812–1827	Tory
George Canning	1827	Tory
Viscount Goderich	1827–1828	Tory
Duke of Wellington	1828–1830	Tory
Earl Grey	1830–1834	Whig
Viscount Melbourne	1834	Whig
Sir Robert Peel	1834–1835	Tory
Viscount Melbourne	1835–1841	Whig
Sir Robert Peel	1841–1846	Tory
Lord John Russell	1846–1852	Whig
Earl of Derby	1852	Tory
Earl of Aberdeen	1852–1855	Peelite
Viscount Palmerston	1855–1858	Liberal
Earl of Derby	1858–1859	Conservative
Viscount Palmerston	1859–1865	Liberal
Earl Russell	1865–1866	Liberal

Earl of Derby	1866–1868	Conservative
Benjamin Disraeli	1868	Conservative
William Gladstone	1868–1874	Liberal
Benjamin Disraeli	1874–1880	Conservative
William Gladstone	1880–1885	Liberal
Marquess of Salisbury	1885–1886	Conservative
William Gladstone	1886	Liberal
Marquess of Salisbury	1886–1892	Conservative
William Gladstone	1892–1894	Liberal
Earl of Rosebery	1894–1895	Liberal
Marquess of Salisbury	1895–1902	Conservative
Arthur Balfour	1902–1905	Conservative
Sir Henry Campbell-Bannerman	1905–1908	Liberal
Herbert Asquith	1908–1915	Liberal
Herbert Asquith	1915–1916	Coalition
David Lloyd-George	1916–1922	Coalition
Andrew Bonar Law	1922–1923	Conservative
Stanley Baldwin	1923–1924	Conservative
James Ramsay MacDonald	1924	Labour
Stanley Baldwin	1924–1929	Conservative
James Ramsay MacDonald	1929–1931	Labour
James Ramsay MacDonald	1931–1935	National Coalition
Stanley Baldwin	1935–1937	National Coalition
Neville Chamberlain	1937–1940	National Coalition
Winston Churchill	1940–1945	Coalition
Winston Churchill	1945	Conservative
Clement Atlee	1945–1951	Labour
Sir Winston Churchill	1951–1955	Conservative
Sir Anthony Eden	1955–1957	Conservative
Harold Macmillan	1957–1963	Conservative
Sir Alec Douglas-Home	1963–1964	Conservative
Harold Wilson	1964–1970	Labour
Edward Heath	1970–1974	Conservative
Harold Wilson	1974–1976	Labour
James Callaghan	1976–1979	Labour
Margaret Thatcher	1979–1990	Conservative
John Major	1990–	Conservative

HOLY ROMAN EMPERORS

Dates given are period of reign.

Charlemagne	800–814		
Louis I (the Pious)	814–840	Lothair I	840–855

Saxon dynasty

Otto I, the Great	936–973	Otto III	983–1002
Otto II	973–983	Henry II	1002–1024

Franconian dynasty

Conrad II	1024–1039	Henry V	1106–1125
Henry III	1039–1056	Lothair III, Duke of Saxony	1125–1137
Henry IV	1056–1106		

Hohenstaufen dynasty

Conrad III	1138–1152	Otto IV of Brunswick	1198–1212
Frederick I, Barbarossa	1152–1190	Frederick II	1212–1250
Henry VI	1190–1197	Conrad IV	1250–1254
Philip of Swabia	1197–1208		

Interregnum
Electors gain power   1254–1273

Transition period

Rudolf I of Habsburg	1273–1292	Frederick of Austria (co-regent)	1314–1322
Adolf of Nassau	1292–1298	Charles IV, of Luxembourg	1347–1378
Albert I, King of Germany	1298–1308	Wenceslas of Luxembourg	1378–1400
Henry VII of Luxembourg	1308–1314	Rupert, Duke of Palatine	1400–1410
Louis IV of Bavaria (co-regent)	1314–1347	Sigismund of Luxembourg	1410–1434

Habsburg dynasty

Albert II	1437–1439	Leopold I	1658–1705
Frederick III	1440–1493	Joseph I	1705–1711
Maximilian I	1493–1519	Charles VI	1711–1740
Charles V, King of Spain	1519–1556	War of Austrian Succession	1740–1748
Ferdinand I	1556–1564	Charles VII of Bavaria	1742–1745
Maximilian II	1564–1576	Francis I of Lorriane	1745–1765
Rudolf II	1576–1612	Joseph II	1765–1790
Matthias	1612–1619	Leopold II	1790–1792
Ferdinand II	1619–1637	Francis II	1792–1806
Ferdinand III	1637–1657		

HABSBURG EMPERORS OF AUSTRIA

Francis II	1804–1835	Francis Joseph	1848–1916
Ferdinand	1835–1848	Charles	1916–1918

HOHENZOLLERN EMPERORS OF GERMANY

William I (of Prussia)	1871–1888	William II	1888–1918
Frederick III	1888		

RULERS OF GERMANY

Weimar Republic

Friedrich Ebert	1919–1925	Paul von Hindenburg	1925–1934

Third Reich
Adolf Hitler   1934–1945

Post World War II
Germany under Allied control   1945–1949

CHANCELLORS OF THE FEDERAL REPUBLIC OF GERMANY (WEST GERMANY)

Konrad Adenauer	1949–1963	Willy Brandt	1969–1974
Dr. Ludwig Erhard	1963–1966	Helmut Schmidt	1974–1982
Kurt Georg Kiesinger	1966–1969	Helmut Kohl	1982–1990

CHAIRMEN OF THE DEMOCRATIC REPUBLIC OF GERMANY (EAST GERMANY)

Walter Ulbricht	1949–1971	Egon Krenz	1989–1990
Erich Honecker	1971–1989		

CHANCELLORS OF UNITED GERMANY

Helmut Kohl   1990–

RULERS OF FRANCE

The Carolingians

Charles I, the Bald	843–877	Charles II	885–888
Louis II	877–879	Eudes	888–898
Louis III	879–882	Charles III	898–922

Robert	922–923	Lothair	954–986
Rudolph	923–936	Louis V	986–987
Louis IV	936–954		

The Capets

Hugh Capet	987–996	Louis VIII	1223–1226
Robert II, the Pious	996–1031	Louis IX	1226–1270
Henry I	1031–1060	Philip III	1270–1285
Philip I	1060–1108	Philip IV	1285–1314
Louis VI	1108–1137	Louis X	1314–1316
Louis VII	1137–1180	Philip V	1316–1322
Philip II	1180–1233	Charles IV	1322–1328

House of Valois

Philip VI	1328–1350	Louis XII	1498–1515
John II	1350–1364	Francis I	1515–1547
Charles V	1364–1380	Henry II	1547–1559
Charles VI	1380–1422	Francis II	1559–1560
Charles VII	1422–1461	Charles IX	1560–1574
Louis XI	1461–1483	Henry III	1574–1589
Charles VIII	1483–1498		

House of Bourbon

Henry IV, of Navarre	1589–1610	Louis XV	1715–1774
Louis XIII	1610–1643	Louis XVI	1774–1793
Louis XIV	1643–1715		

The First Republic and First Empire

Napoleon Bonaparte (first consul)	1799–1804	Napoleon I (emperor)	1804–1814

Restoration of monarchy

Louis XVIII	1814–1824	Louis-Philippe	1830–1848
Charles X	1824–1830		

Second Republic

Louis Napoleon Bonaparte (president)	1848–1852	Napoleon III (emperor)	1852–1870

Third Republic

Louis Adolphe Thiers	1871–1873	Paul Deschanel	1920
Marshal Patrice de MacMahon	1873–1879	Alexandre Millerand	1920–1924
Paul Grévy	1879–1887	Gaston Doumergue	1924–1931
Marie Carnot	1887–1894	Albert Lebrun	1932–1940
Jean Casimir-Périer	1894–1895		
François Faure	1895–1899	Vichy government (under Germans)	1940–1944
Émile Loubet	1899–1906		
Armand C. Fallières	1906–1913	Provisional government	1944–1946
Raymond Poincaré	1913–1920		

Fourth Republic

Vincent Auriol	1947–1954	René Coty	1954–1959

Fifth Republic

Charles de Gaulle	1959–1969	Valéry Giscard d'Estaing	1974–1981
Georges Pompidou	1969–1974	François Mitterrand	1981–

RULERS OF SPAIN

Habsburg dynasty

Charles I (V of Germany)	1516–1556		
Philip II	1556–1598	Philip IV	1621–1665
Philip III	1598–1621	Charles II	1665–1700

Bourbon dynasty

Philip V	1700–1724	Charles IV	1788–1808
Louis I	1724	Joseph Bonaparte	1808–1814
Philip V (restored)	1724–1746	Ferdinand II	1814–1833
Ferdinand VI	1746–1759	Isabella II	1833–1868
Charles II	1759–1788		

Other monarchs

Amadeus of Savoy	1870–1873

First republic   **1873–1874**

Restoration of Monarchy

Alfonso XII	1874–1885	Alfonso XIII	1886–1931
Primo de Rivero (dictator)	1923–1930		

Second Republic

Niceto Alcalá Zamora	1931–1936	General Francisco Franco	1939–1975
Manuel Azaña	1936–1939		

Restoration of monarchy

Juan Carlos	1975–

Prime ministers

Admiral Luis Blanco	1973	Adolfo Suárez	1976–1982
Carlos Navarro	1973–1976	Felipe González	1982–

PERIODS OF JAPAN

Yamato	c. 300–592	
Asaka	592–710	Empress Suiko (592–628)
		Emperor Temmu (673–686)
Nara	710–794	Emperor Kammu (781–806)
Heian	794–1185	Japan ruled from Heian (now called Kyoto)
Fujiwara	858–1160	Fujiwara clan rules
Taira	1159–1185	Taira clan take control
Kamakura	1185–1333	Minamoto Yoritomo defeats Taira clan; in 1192 he becomes shogun
Namboku	1334–1392	End of shogun rule in 1333; Emperor Godaigo rules alone 1333–1339; imperial line splits into northern and southern courts
Ashikaga	1338–1573	Ashikaga Takauji becomes shogun in 1338
Muromachi	1392–1573	Two rival courts are unified
Sengoku	1467–1600	Emperor Gonara (1527–1557)
Momoyama	1573–1603	Oda Nobunaga, a daimyo (baron), deposes the shogun and becomes dictator to 1582
Edo	1603–1867	Ieyasu Tokugawa becomes shogun in 1603; Tokugawa shoguns rule until 1867
Meiji	1868–1912	Emperor Mutsuhito (Meiji) is restored; he ends the shogunate and modernizes Japan
Taisho	1912–1926	Emperor Yoshihito
Showa	1926–1989	Emperor Hirohito
Heisei	1989–	Emperor Akihoto

TSARS OF RUSSIA

Ivan III, the Great	1462–1505	Basil (IV) Shuiski	1606–1610
Basil III	1505–1533	(Interregnum	1610–1613)
Ivan IV, the Terrible	1533–1584	Michael Romanov	1613–1645
Fyodor I	1584–1598	Alexis	1645–1676
Boris Godunov	1598–1605	Fyodor III	1676–1682
Fyodor II	1605	Ivan V & Peter I, the Great	1682–1689
Demetrius	1605–1606	Peter I	1689–1725

Catherine I	1725–1727	Paul I	1796–1801
Peter II	1727–1730	Alexander I	1801–1825
Anna	1730–1740	Nicholas I	1825–1855
Ivan VI	1740–1741	Alexander II	1855–1881
Elizabeth	1741–1762	Alexander III	1881–1894
Peter III	1762	Nicholas II	1894–1917
Catherine II, the Great	1762–1796		

EFFECTIVE RULERS OF THE UNION OF SOVIET SOCIALIST REPUBLICS

Vladimir Lenin	1917–1922	Yuri Andropov	1982–1984
Joseph Stalin	1922–1953	Konstantin Chernenko	1984–1985
Nikita Khrushchev	1953–1964	Mikhail Gorbachev	1985–1992
Leonid Brezhnev	1964–1982		

PRESIDENTS OF RUSSIA

| Boris Yeltsin | 1992– |

PRESIDENTS OF THE UNITED STATES OF AMERICA

George Washington	1789–1797	None
John Adams	1797–1801	Federalist
Thomas Jefferson	1801–1809	Democratic-Republican
James Madison	1809–1817	Democratic-Republican
James Monroe	1817–1825	Democratic-Republican
John Quincy Adams	1825–1829	Democratic-Republican
Andrew Jackson	1829–1837	Democratic
Martin Van Buren	1837–1841	Democratic
William H. Harrison	1841	Whig
John Tyler	1841–1845	Whig
James K. Polk	1845–1849	Democratic
Zachary Taylor	1849–1850	Whig
Millard Fillmore	1850–1853	Whig
Franklin Pierce	1853–1857	Democratic
James Buchanan	1857–1861	Democratic
Abraham Lincoln	1861–1865	Republican
Andrew Johnson	1865–1869	National Union
Ulysses S. Grant	1869–1877	Republican
Rutherford Hayes	1877–1881	Republican
James Garfield	1881	Republican
Chester Arthur	1881–1885	Republican
Grover Cleveland	1885–1889	Democratic
Benjamin Harrison	1889–1893	Republican
Grover Cleveland	1893–1897	Democratic
William McKinley	1897–1901	Republican
Theodore Roosevelt	1901–1909	Republican
William Taft	1909–1913	Republican
Woodrow Wilson	1913–1921	Democratic
Warren Harding	1921–1923	Republican
Calvin Coolidge	1923–1929	Republican
Herbert Hoover	1929–1933	Republican
Franklin D. Roosevelt	1933–1945	Democratic
Harry S. Truman	1945–1953	Democratic
Dwight Eisenhower	1953–1961	Republican
John F. Kennedy	1961–1963	Democratic
Lyndon Johnson	1963–1969	Democratic
Richard Nixon	1969–1974	Republican
Gerald Ford	1974–1977	Republican
Jimmy Carter	1977–1981	Democratic
Ronald Reagan	1981–1989	Republican
George Bush	1989–1993	Republican
Bill Clinton	1993–	Democratic

PRIME MINISTERS OF CANADA

Sir John MacDonald	1867–1873	William King	1926–1930
Alexander MacKenzie	1873–1878	Richard Bennett	1930–1935
Sir John MacDonald	1878–1891	William King	1935–1948
Sir John Abbott	1891–1892	Louis St Laurent	1948–1957
Sir John Thompson	1892–1894	John Diefenbaker	1957–1963
Sir Mackenzie Bowell	1894–1896	Lester Pearson	1963–1968
Sir Charles Tupper	1896	Pierre Trudeau	1968–1979
Sir Wilfrid Laurier	1896–1911	Charles Clark	1979–1980
Sir Robert Borden	1911–1920	Pierre Trudeau	1980–1984
Arthur Meighen	1920–1921	John Turner	1984
William King	1921–1926	Martin Mulroney	1984–
Arthur Meighen	1926		

PRIME MINISTERS OF AUSTRALIA

Australia was established as a Commonwealth in 1901.

Sir Edmund Barton	1901–1903	Sir Robert Menzies	1939–1941
Alfred Deakin	1903–1904	Sir Arthur Fadden	1941
John Watson	1904	John Curtin	1941–1945
Sir George Reid	1904–1905	Francis Forde	1945
Alfred Deakin	1905–1908	Joseph Chifley	1945–1949
Andrew Fisher	1908–1909	Sir Robert Menzies	1949–1966
Alfred Deakin	1909–1910	Harold Holt	1966–1967
Andrew Fisher	1910–1913	Sir John McEwen	1967–1968
Sir Joseph Cook	1913–1914	John Gorton	1968–1971
Andrew Fisher	1914–1915	William McMahon	1971–1972
William Hughes	1915–1923	Edward Gough Whitlam	1972–1975
Stanley Bruce	1923–1929	John Fraser	1975–1983
James Scullin	1929–1932	Robert Hawke	1983–1991
Joseph Lyons	1932–1939	Paul Keating	1991–
Sir Earle Page	1939		

PRIME MINISTERS OF NEW ZEALAND

Sir Joseph Ward	1906–1912	Sir Walter Nash	1957–1960
Thomas MacKenzie	1912–1915	Keith Holyoake	1960–1972
William Massey	1915–1925	Sir John Marshall	1972
Sir Francis Bell	1925	Norman Kirk	1972–1974
Joseph Coates	1925–1928	Hugh Watt	1974
Sir Joseph Ward	1928–1930	Wallace (Bill) Rowling	1974–1975
George Forbes	1930–1935	Robert Muldoon	1975–1984
Michael Savage	1935–1940	David Lange	1984–1989
Peter Fraser	1940–1949	Geoffrey Palmer	1989–1990
Sir Sidney Holland	1949–1957	Michael Moore	1990
Keith Holyoake	1957	James Bolger	1990–

PRESIDENTS OF THE REPUBLIC OF ITALY

Alcide de Gasperi (acting head of state)	1946	Giovanni Leone	1971–1978
Enrico de Nicola (provisional president)	1946–1948	Amintore Fanfani	1978
Luigi Einaudi	1948–1955	Alessandro Pertini	1978–1985
Giovanni Gronchi	1955–1962	Francesco Cossiga	1985–1992
Antonio Segni	1962–1964	Oscar Luigi Scalfaro	1992–
Giuseppe Saragat	1964–1971		

Prime Ministers

Alcide de Gasperi	1946–1953	Adone Zoli	1957–1958
Guiseppe Pella	1953–1954	Amintore Fanfani	1958–1959
Amintore Fanfani	1954	Antonio Segni	1959–1960
Mario Scelba	1954–1955	Fernando Tambroni	1960
Antonio Segni	1955–1957	Amintore Fanfani	1960–1963

Giovanni Leone	1963	Francesco Cossiga	1979–1980
Aldo Moro	1963–1968	Arnaldo Forlani	1980–1981
Giovanni Leone	1968	Giovanni Spadolini	1981–1982
Mariano Rumor	1968–1970	Armintore Fanfani	1982–1983
Emilio Colombo	1970–1972	Bettino Craxi	1983–1987
Giulio Andreotti	1972–1973	Giovanni Goria	1987–1988
Mariano Rumor	1973–1974	Luigi Ciriaco de Mita	1988–1989
Aldo Moro	1974–1976	Giulio Andreotti	1989–
Giulio Andreotti	1976–1979		

PRESIDENTS OF REPUBLIC OF INDIA

Dr. Rajendra Prasad	1949–1962	Basappa Jatti	1977
Dr. Sarvapalli Radhakrishnan	1962–1967	Neelam Reddy	1977–1982
Dr. Zahir Hussain	1967–1969	Giani Zail Singh	1982–1987
Varahgiri Girir	1969–1974	Ramaswamy Venkataraman	1987–
Fakhruddin Ahmed	1974–1977		

Prime Ministers

Jawaharlal Nehru	1949–1964	Charan Singh	1979–1980
Gulzarilal Nanda	1964	Indira Gandhi	1980–1984
Lal Shastri	1964–1966	Rajiv Gandhi	1984–1989
Gulzarilal Nanda	1966	V.P. Singh	1989–1990
Indira Gandhi	1966–1977	Chandra Shekhar	1990–1991
Shri Desai	1977–1979	P.V. Narasimha Rao	1991–

MAJOR WARS

Date	Name of war	Warring parties
c. 1250 B.C.	Trojan wars	Mycenaeans v. Trojans
431–404 B.C.	Peloponnesian War	Athens v. Sparta
264–241 B.C.	First Punic War	
218–101 B.C.	Second Punic War	Rome v. Carthage
149–146 B.C.	Third Punic War	
1096–1099	First Crusade	
1147–1149	Second Crusade	Saracens v. Christians over Palestine
1189–1192	Third Crusade	
1202–1204	Fourth Crusade	
1337–1453	Hundred Years War	England v. France
1455–1485	Wars of the Roses	House of York v. House of Lancaster
1562–1598	French Wars of Religion	Huguenots v. Catholics
1642–1648	English Civil War	Cavaliers v. Roundheads
1618–1648	Thirty Years War	Catholic League (Germany, Austria, Spain) v Denmark, Sweden, France
1689–1697	War of League of Augsburg	France v. the League, England, and the Netherlands
1700	Great Northern War	Sweden v. Russia, Denmark, Poland, Holland
1701–1713	War of Spanish Succession	Spain, France and Bavaria v. England, Holland, Austrian empire and Portugal
1730–1738	War of Polish Succession	Russia, Poland v. France
1740–1748	War of Austrian Succession	Austria, Britain v. Prussia, Bavaria, France, Spain
1756–1763	Seven Years War	Britain and Prussia v. France, Austria, and Russia
1775–1783	Revolutionary War (American)	American colonies v. Britain
1793–1815	Napoleonic wars	France v. Britain, Austria, Sweden, Russia, and Prussia
1821–1829	Greek War of Independence	Greece v. Ottoman Turkey
1846–1848	Mexican–American War	Mexico v. U.S.
1854–1856	Crimean War	Russia v. Britain, France and Turkey
1859	War for Italian Independence	France, Piedmont-Sardinia v. Austria
1861–1865	U.S. Civil War	Confederates v. Unionists
1866	Austro–Prussian War	Prussia v. Austria
1870	Franco–Prussian War	France v. Prussia
1894–1895	Chinese–Japanese War	China v. Japan
1899–1902	Boer War	Britain v. Boers (Dutch) in South Africa
1904–1905	Russo-Japanese War	Russia v. Japan

1914–1918	World War I	Germany and Austria-Hungary v. France, Russia, Britain and other nations
1918–1921	Russian Civil War	Bolsheviks v. White Russians
1931–1933	Chinese–Japanese War	Japan v. China
1936–1939	Spanish Civil War	Nationalists (Franco) v. Republicans
1939–1945	World War II	Britain, France, USSR, U.S.A., and other nations v. Germany, Italy, and Japan
1967	Six Day War	Israel v. Arab states
1950–1953	Korean War	N. Korea v. S. Korea
1964–1973	Vietnam War	N. Vietnam v. S. Vietnam and U.S.A.
1980–1988	Iran–Iraq War	Iran v. Iraq

EXPLORATION AND DISCOVERY

Place	Achievement	Explorer	Date
World	circumnavigated	Ferdinand Magellan (Portuguese for Spain)	1519–1521
Pacific Ocean	discovered	Vasco Nuñcz dc Balboa (Spanish)	1513

Africa

River Congo (mouth)	discovered	Diogo Cão (Portuguese)	c. 1483
Cape of Good Hope	sailed round	Bartolomeu Diaz (Portuguese)	1488
River Niger	explored	Mungo Park (British)	1795
River Zambezi	discovered	David Livingstone (British)	1851
Sudan	explored	Heinrich Barth (German for Britain)	1852–1855
Victoria Falls	discovered	Livingstone	1855
Lake Tanganyika	discovered	Richard Burton and John Speke (British)	1858
River Congo	traced	Sir Henry Stanley (British)	1877

Asia

China	visited	Marco Polo (Italian)	c. 1272
Asia, India (Africa)	explored	Cheng Ho (Chinese)	1405–1433
India (Cape route)	visited	Vasco da Gama (Portuguese)	1498
Japan	visited	St. Francis-Xavier (Spanish)	1549
China	explored	Ferdinand Richthofen (German)	1868

North and Central America

North America	settled	Leif Ericsson (Norse)	c. 1003
Caribbean	discovered	Christopher Colombus (Italian for Spain)	1492
Newfoundland	discovered	John Cabot (Italian for England)	1497
Central America	explored	Rodrigo de Bastidas (Spanish)	1501
Mexico	conquered	Hernando Cortés (Spanish)	1519–21
St. Lawrence River	explored	Jacques Cartier (French)	1534–1536
Mississippi River	discovered	Hernando de Soto (Spanish)	1541
Canadian interior	explored	Samuel de Champlain (French)	1603–1609
Hudson Bay	discovered	Henry Hudson (English)	1610
Alaska	discovered	Vitus Bering (Danish for Russia)	1728

South America

South America	visited	Columbus	1498
Venezuela	explored	Alonso de Ojeda (Spanish)	1499
Brazil	discovered	Pedro Alvares Cabral (Portuguese)	1500
Tierra del Fuego	discovered	Magellan	1520
Peru	conquered	Francisco Pizarro (Spanish)	1530–1538
River Amazon	explored	Francisco de Orellana (Spanish)	1541
Cape Horn	discovered	Willem Schouten (Dutch)	1616

Australasia, Polar regions etc.

Greenland	visited	Eric the Red (Norse)	c. 982
Spitsbergen	discovered	Willem Barents (Dutch)	1596
Tasmania	visited	Abel Tasman (Dutch)	1642
New Zealand	sighted	Tasman	1642
New Zealand	visited	James Cook (British)	1769
Antarctica	sighted	Nathaniel Palmer (American)	1820

Antarctica	circumnavigated	Fabian von Bellingshausen (Russian)	1819–1821
Australian	explored	Charles Wilkes (American)	c. 1838–1842
Australia	crossed (S–N)	Robert Burke (Irish) and William Wills (British)	
Greenland	explored	Fridtjof Nansen (Norwegian)	1888
North Pole	reached	Robert Peary (American)	1909
South Pole	reached	Roald Amundsen (Norwegian)	1911
Antarctica	crossed	Sir Vivian Fuchs (British)	1957–1958

Space

Earth	orbited	Yuri Gagarin (Russian)	1961
Moon	visited	Neil Armstrong (American)	1969

UNITED NATIONS MEMBER COUNTRIES

Country	Joined		
Afghanistan	1946	Ecuador	1945
Albania	1955	Egypt	1945
Algeria	1962	El Salvador	1945
Angola	1976	Equatorial Guinea	1968
Antigua and Barbuda	1981	Estonia	1991
Argentina	1945	Ethiopia	1945
Armenia	1992	Fiji	1970
Azerbaijan	1992	Finland	1955
Australia	1945	France	1945
Austria	1955	Gabon	1960
Bahamas	1973	Gambia	1965
Bahrain	1971	Germany	1973
Bangladesh	1974	Ghana	1957
Barbados	1966	Greece	1945
Belarus	1945	Grenada	1974
Belgium	1945	Guatemala	1945
Belize	1981	Guinea	1958
Benin	1960	Guinea-Bissau	1974
Bhutan	1971	Guyana	1966
Bolivia	1945	Haiti	1945
Bosnia-Herzegovina	1992	Honduras	1945
Botswana	1966	Hungary	1955
Brazil	1945	Iceland	1946
Brunei	1984	India	1945
Bulgaria	1955	Indonesia	1950
Burkina Faso	1960	Iran	1945
Burundi	1962	Iraq	1945
Cambodia	1955	Ireland, Republic of	1955
Cameroon	1960	Israel	1949
Canada	1945	Italy	1955
Cape Verde	1975	Ivory Coast	1960
Central African Republic	1960	Jamaica	1962
Chad	1960	Japan	1956
Chile	1945	Jordan	1955
China	1945	Kazakhstan	1992
Colombia	1945	Kenya	1963
Comoros	1975	Korea, DPR	1991
Congo	1960	Korea, Republic of	1991
Costa Rica	1945	Kuwait	1963
Croatia	1992	Kirghizia	1992
Cuba	1945	Laos	1955
Cyprus	1960	Latvia	1991
Czechoslovakia	1945	Lebanon	1945
Denmark	1945	Lesotho	1966
Djibouti	1977	Liberia	1945
Dominica	1978	Libya	1955
Dominican Republic	1945	Liechtenstein	1990

Lithuania	1991	St Vincent & the Grenadines	1980
Luxembourg	1945	Sao Tome & Principe	1975
Madagascar	1960	Saudi Arabia	1945
Malawi	1964	Senegal	1960
Malaysia	1957	Seychelles	1976
Maldives, Republic of	1965	Sierra Leone	1961
Mali	1960	Singapore	1965
Malta	1964	Slovenia	1992
Marshall Islands	1991	Solomon Islands	1978
Mauritania	1961	Somali Republic	1960
Mauritius	1968	South Africa	1945
Mexico	1945	Spain	1955
Micronesia	1991	Sri Lanka	1955
Moldova	1992	Sudan	1956
Mongolian PR	1961	Surinam	1975
Morocco	1956	Swaziland	1968
Mozambique	1975	Sweden	1946
Myanmar	1948	Syria	1945
Namibia	1990	Tadzhikstan	1992
Nepal	1955	Tanzania	1961
Netherlands	1945	Thailand	1946
New Zealand	1945	Togo	1960
Nicaragua	1945	Trinidad & Tobago	1962
Niger	1960	Tunisia	1956
Nigeria	1960	Turkmenistan	1992
Norway	1945	Turkey	1945
Oman	1971	Uganda	1962
Pakistan	1947	Ukraine	1945
Panama	1945	United Arab Emirates	1971
Papua New Guinea	1975	United Kingdom	1945
Paraguay	1945	United States	1945
Peru	1945	Uruguay	1945
Philippines	1945	Uzbekistan	1992
Poland	1945	Vanuatu	1981
Portugal	1955	Venezuela	1945
Qatar	1971	Vietnam	1977
Romania	1955	Western Samoa	1976
Russia	1945	Yemen (as separate states)	1947 and 1967
Rwanda	1962	Yugoslavia	1945
San Marino	1992	Zaire	1960
St Kitts-Nevis	1983	Zambia	1964
St Lucia	1979	Zimbabwe	1980

Index

This index has been designed to help you find easily the information you are looking for. You may find that the subject you are interested in has no article to itself but is mentioned in several places. For example, the start of radio can be found on a Communications special and later on, early radios in the home can be found on a People special. Page numbers in **boldface type** (heavy and dark) indicate where the main reference to a subject can be found. Page numbers in *italic type* (slanting) refer to pages on which there are illustrations. Take the entry on

Alexander the Great for example:
Alexander the Great 77, 78, 79, 86, **90–91**, 94, 138, *154*, 155
The main entry on Alexander is on pages 90 to 91. On page 154 is an illustration of the battle formation he used with great success. On the other pages listed you will find information in the main or boxed text or in the timeline about his victories, his successors, and the effect his actions had on spreading Greek culture and thought throughout the ancient world.

farming 268, **323**
calendar 293
government 300, 380
and the *conquistadores* 318, 320, 358, 362–363, *362*, 366
arts and crafts 324
writing 342
conversion to Christianity 364, *364*
human sacrifices 323, *365*
warriors 394
Azura Mazda 75, *75*

B

Babbage, Charles 551, *613*
Babur, Emperor of India 319, *321*, *348*, 350, **360**, *360–361*, 361, *360*, 395
Babylon 25, **47**, **70–71**
 Hittites conquer 11, 39
 origins of 34
 rise of empire 40
 religion *44*
 wars with Assyrians 50, 58, 67, 69
 Aramaeans overrun 55
 Hanging Gardens **71**, *71*, 73
 Persians conquer 74
 and Alexander the Great 91
 Seleucid dynasty 94
Bac-Ninh, battle of (1884) *605*
Bach, Johann Sebastian *485*, *491*, 494
Backstaffs 339, *339*
Bacon, Francis 447
Bacon, Roger 270, 273, 293
Bactria 94
Baden-Powell, Robert 630
Badoglio, Marshal 696, 704
Baekeland, Leo *613*
Bagauda, King of Kano 217
Baghdad 192, 212
 founded 159, 213
 part of Islamic empire *176*
 Abbasid dynasty 186, 190–191
 trade 228
 in Seljuk empire 230
 Tamerlane conquers 302
 Suleiman I conquers 319
 Ottoman Turks capture 363, 399, 430
 World War I 651
Baghdad Railway 626
Bahadur Khan *361*
Bahamas 433, 714
Bahrain 33
Baird, John Logie *661*, 670
Bakari 345
Balaklava, battle of (1854) *577*, *577*, 579
Balboa, Vasco Nuñez de 353
Baldwin IV, King of Jerusalem 234
Baldwin of Bouillon 232
Balfour Declaration (1917) 639, 651, 710
Balkan League 634–635
Balkan Pact 681
Balkan Wars 634–635, 636
Balkans 35, 375, 455, 636, 666
 see also individual countries
Ball, John 298, 299
Ballet *484*, 566, *646*
Ballets Russes 630

Balliol, Edward 286
Balliol, John 274, *274*, *275*, 279
Balloons *500*, 501, 519, *632*
Balthasar Carlos, Prince of Spain *423*
Baltic Sea 288–289, 388, 466–467
Baltimore *539*
Ban Chao, General 121, 122, 126
Bangkok 519
Bangladesh *708*, 714, 719, 733, 742
 see also India and Pakistan
Bank of England 465, *465*, 468, 469, 552, 704
Banking 257, *257*, 308, *309*
Banknotes 440, 469, *469*, 532, 548
Bannister, Roger 722
Bannockburn, battle of (1314) 275, *275*, 283
Bantu people, 10, 78, *103*, 182, 195
Banyan trees *96*
Barbados 418, 714
Barbarians 77, 113, 140, **142–145**, 156
Barbarossa 359
Barcelona 438, 501, 605, 679, 683, 693
Barcelona, Treaty of (1529) 361
Barents, William *341*
Barmecide family 190, 192
Barnet, battle of (1471) 329
Barometers 453
Barons 225, 262–263, 267
Baroque style 404, 412, 492
Barrie, J. M. 626
Barrows 31
Basil, Emperor 201
Basil III, Tsar 350
Basil IV Shuisky, Tsar 407, 408
Basques 190, 687, 736, 737
Bastille, Paris 522
Batavia (Djakarta) 399, 414, 424, 426, *426*, 454, 539
Bath *493*
Baths and bathing *117*, 434, *435*, *517*
Batu Khan 264
Bauhaus 654, 655
Bavaria 190, 408, 433, 667
Bay of Pigs 726
Bayeux *221*, 312
Bayeux Tapestry *5*, *222*
Bayonets 437, 472
Bayonne 437
Beachy Head, battle of (1690) *463*
Beacons *342*
The Beatles 729
Beauvoir, Simone de 714
Becket, Thomas à 238, 248–249, *249*, 251
Bede, the Venerable 169, *180*, *181*, 184
Bedford, John, Duke of 304, 307
Bee hives *189*
"Beehive" tombs 40–41, *40*
Beethoven, Ludwig van 484, 536, 551
Behaim, Martin 340
Behn, Aphra 405, 455
Beijing (Peking):
 Kublai Khan builds 270, 272
 Forbidden City **294**, *294*

Imperial City 294, 295
 Observatory *295*
 becomes capital of China 307
 Manchus occupy 432
 Temple of Heaven *481*, *493*
 British occupy 583
 Boxer Rebellion 622, *622*
 Japan captures 639, *686*, 687
 communists capture 716
 Tiananmen Square massacre 719, *735*, 742, *742*
Belgium:
 permanent neutrality 565
 famine 571
 "scramble for Africa" 598
 and the Congo 630
 World War I 642–643
 World War II 693, 694
 see also Austrian Netherlands, Spanish Netherlands
Belgrade 358, 458, 463, 502
Belisarius *142*, 162, 167
Belize 714
Bell, Alexander Graham 589, *589*, 596
Bell Telephone Company *690*
Belsharusur (Belshazzar) 71
Ben-Gurion, David 710, **711**, *711*
Benedict, St. *166*, 167, 197
Benedict XI, Pope 281
Benedict XII, Pope 286
Benedict XIII, antipope 302
Benedictines 167, 169, 197
Bengal 96, 257, 361, 386, 424, 494, 495, *528*, 608, 628
Benghazi 638; 741
Benin 238, *246*, **280–281**, *321*, 345, *404*, 462, *462*
Benin City 280
Benz, Karl 609
Berbers 176, 184, 192–193, 248, 344
Bergman, Ingrid 696
Bering, Vitus 478, 497
Bering Strait *13*, 18, 62, 497
Berlin: 474, 588
 1848 uprising 571
 Spartakist uprising 656
 Olympic games (1936) 682, 698
 Berlin Airlift 638, *701*, 710, 744
 Berlin Wall 718, 726, 739, *739*
Berlin, Congress of (1878) 599
Berlin Academy of Sciences 466, 504
Berlin Conference (1884) 558, 599, *599*
Bern 332, 391
Bernard, St 242
Bernicia 194
Bernini, Giovanni *405*, 412, 413, 417, 423, 446
Bernstein, Leonard 725
Berry, Duke of 277, *299*, 326
Bessemer, Henry 579, *613*
Bethlehem 118, 129
Beveridge Report 699
Bevin, Ernest *701*
Bhagavad Gita 97
Bhutto, Benazir 719, 742

Biafra 718, 729, 730, 731, 733
Bible 6, 8, 50, 57, 246, 299, 312, 313, *406*, 411, *444*, 445, 446
Bicycles *589*
Big Bang theory 710
Bihar 257
Bikini atoll 704
Bilbao 683
Bill of Rights (1689) 458–459, 463, 526
Birdseye, Clarence 675, 707
Biro, Laszlo 688, 690
Birth control 648, *743*
Bishops' wars 430
Bismarck, Otto von 583, 586, 592, **593**, *593*, 601, 611
Bison 620–621, *621*
Bithynia 110
Bizet, Georges 596
Bjarni Herjolfsson 217, 218
Black-and-Tans 649, 663
Black Death 238, 240, 269, 288, **290–291**, 298
"Black Hole of Calcutta" 510
Black civil rights: 586, 619, 718, 722, 725
 Ku Klux Klan and 585, 586
 in the 19th century 614
 apartheid 638, 699, 714, 741, 742, 744
 Black power *698*, 718
 race riots 729, 730
Black Sea 141, 148, 162, 218, 336, 466, 478, 519, 526, 569, 576–577, 636
Blackbeard *450*
Blackheath 299
Blake, William *504*
Blanche of Castile 263
"Blanketeers" 547
Blenheim, battle of (1704) *470*, 471, 474
Blenheim Palace 413
Blériot, Louis 630
Bliddhagupta, Emperor 151
Blitzkrieg 692, 694
Block printing 312, *313*
Blois, Treaty of (1505) 350
Blondel 257
Blood River, battle of (1838) 565
"Bloody Sunday" (1972) 733
Bloomer, Amelia Jenks 572
Blücher, Gebhard von 542, *542*
Blue Mosque, Istanbul *412*, 414
Blum, Leon 682
Boccaccio, Giovanni 247, 291
Bocchi, Dorotea 279
Bodleian Library, Oxford 413
Body paint 195
Boer wars 558, 564–565, *564*, 599, 601, 623, 626
Boers 478, 558, 562, **564–565**, 576, 579, 616
Bogart, Humphrey 696
Bohemia 195, *200*, **201**, 207, 209, 416, 423
Bohemund of Otranto 232
Bojador, Cape 261, 306, 307, 310
Bokhara 230, 263, 586

welfare state 685, 699, 714
appeasement 687
World War II 692, 693, 694–697
end of World War II 700
Berlin Airlift 710
Commonwealth **714–715**
immigration 726
Suez crisis 725, 733
and the EEC 726, 729
Northern Ireland troubles 733
joins EEC 734
Falklands War 718, 738
rulers of Britain 749–751
prime ministers of Britain 751–752
see also Northern Ireland; Scotland; Wales
Britain, battle of (1940) 694, **695**, 713
British Army *633*
British Columbia 593
British empire 610–611, 714
see also Britain
British Museum 455, 545
British North American Act (1867) 587, *587*
British Petroleum *706*
British South Africa Company 616
British Union of Fascists 699
Brittany 30–31, 296
Brodars 225
Brodgar, Ring of 39
Brontë, Charlotte 571
Brontë, Emily 571
Bronze Age 11, 31, 39, 40, 52, *53*
Bronze work 43, *280–281*, *404*
Brooke, Sir James 559, 569
Brooke, Rupert 645
Brooklyn 648
Brown, Sir Arthur Whitten 690
Brown, John 581
Brown, Lancelot "Capability" 493
Browning, John M. *633*
Bruce, Robert 274–275
Brueghel, Pieter 324
Bruges, Truce of (1375) 296
Brunanburth, battle of (937) 209
Brunei 569, 714
Brunel, Isambard Kingdom 574
Brunelleschi, Filippo 253, *335*
Bruno, Giordano 373
Brusilov, General 648
Brussels 701, *729*
Brutus 115, 118
Bubonic plague 290, 442
Bucharest 648
Bucharest, Treaty of (1913) 609
Buchenwald *694*
Buckingham, Duke of 417
Buckingham Palace, London 413
Bucklers *497*
Budapest 571
Buddha 11, **64**, *64*, 73, *81*, 96, *125*, 136, *205*, *229*
Buddhism:
in China 115, 122, 159, 170, 174, 204, *205*, *365*

in India 96–97, 124, 125, 136–137
in Japan 144, 159, 168, 171, **199**, 204, *365*, *393*
in Korea 143
monks 169
spread of 157, 204, 284, *284*
stupas *97*
wheel of life *137*
Buenos Aires 366
Buffalo 539
Buganda 478, 480, 532
Buildings *see* Architecture
Bulgaria:
in Ottoman empire 239, 295, 302
independence 558, 599, 630
Balkan Wars 634–635
becomes communist state 701, 703
collapse of communism 739
Bulgars 182, **184–185**, 201
Bull Run, battle of (1861) 582
Bunker Hill, battle of (1775) *480*, *518*
Bunsen burners 579
Bunyan, John 405
Bureau of Freed Slaves 584
Burgundy 167, 214, 291, 307, 326, 370
Burgundy, Duke of 326
Burke, Robert O'Hara *631*
Burma:
trade 259
Mongol invasions 274, 279
Konbaung dynasty 479, 510
Anglo-Burmese Wars 515, 559, 576, 609
British colony 604
World War II 696, 697
independence 709, 715
see also Myanmar
"Burning of the Books," China 99
Bursa 286
Burton, Sir Richard 596
Busch, Wilhelm 584
Bush, George 718
Bushmen 103
Bushnell, David 555
Byrd, Richard 672
Byrhtnoth of Essex 214
Byron, Lord 552, *552*
Byzantine empire 157, 158, **162–163**
arts and crafts 164
under Justinian 167
spread of 168
wars with Persia 168, 174, 177
Arab incursions 176
Iconoclast movement 184
wars with Bulgars 184
clothes 196
government 220
war with Seljuk empire 231, 234
decline 237, 279, 292
fall of Constantinople 302–303, 312, 315, 317, 331
Byzantium 70, 136, 141, 162, 302
see also Constantinople

C

Cabot, John 318, 340–341, *341*, 344
Cabot, Sebastian 350
Cabral, Pedro 339, 346
Cadillac, Antoine de la Mothe 471
Cadiz 57, 391
Caernarvon Castle *237*, 273
Caesar, Julius 6–7, 78, 95, *95*, 112, **115**, *115*, 118, 396
Caesarion 95
Cahokia 182
Cairo 158, 212, 355, 593
Calais 286, 288, 305, 312, 375
Calais, battle of (1347) 304
Calcutta 399, 425, 463, 502, 510, 528, *528*, 545
Calendars:
Julian 115, 396
Aztec 293
Gregorian 391, **396**, 510
Revolutionary *541*
Calicut 339, 353
California 366, 563, 571, 572, 614, 616–617, *616*, 678
Caligula, Emperor 121
Calistus III, Pope 337
Calligraphy 164, *164*, 485
Calvin, John 354–355, *354*, 363, 366, 377, 379, 383
Camargo, Marie-Anne de Cupis de *484*
Cambodia:
Khmer empire 159, 240, *241*, **310–311**
French colony 584, 604
independence from France 703, 714
Vietnam invades 719, 737
Khmer Rouge **726**, 734, 737
and the Vietnam War 733
Cambrai, Peace of (1529) 361
Cambridge, Massachusetts 421
Cambyses, King of Persia 74
Camels 180, *193*, 229
Cameras *661*
Campbell, Sir Archibald *514*
Campbell clan 459
Camus, Albert 709
Canaan 39, 49, 50, 56
Canada:
Ice Age 12
explorers 318, 341, 366
first settlers 410–411
Province of New France formed 443
wars between British and French 498–499
divided into British and French-speaking territories 526
War of 1812 **538–539**
in British empire 557, 580
unification 557, 558, 565
revolt against British rule 562
becomes a Dominion **586–587**
Red River rebellion 590
gold rushes 616, 617
World War I 644, 656
independence 611, 715, *715*

in the Commonwealth 714, 715
Quebec independence campaign 737
prime ministers of 756
see also North America
Canadian Pacific Railway 586, 587, 609
Canals:
in China *161*, 170, *170*, 181, *181*, 189
in Europe *501*
Canary Islands 281
Canberra 639, 672, 699, *715*
Cannae, battle of (216 B.C.) 98, 106
Canned food *509*, 536, *625*
Cannon 314, *314*, 366, 394, *632*
Cano, Juan Sebastian del 341
Canoe 52, 76, *152*
Canopic jars *26*
Canossa *211*, 231
Canterbury 217
Canterbury Cathedral *221*, *249*
Canton 427, *503*, 667, 688
Canute, King of England and Denmark 158, 218, 222, **223**, *223*
Canute IV, King of Denmark 231, 232
Cao, Diego 339
Cape Colony 478, 536, 564–565, 576, 596
Cape Town 398
Cape Verde Islands 353
Capet, Hugh 214–215, *215*
Capetian dynasty 214–215
Capetown 438
Capitol (building), Washington DC 552
Capone, Al 670, *670*
Cappadocia 39, 131
Capua 94
Capuchin friars 368, 398, 433
Caracalla, Emperor 131
Carausius 135
Caravaggio, Michelangelo 384
Caravansaries *261*
Caravel *306–307*
Carberry, battle of (1567) 377
Carcemish, battle of (605 B.C.) 70
Cardinals 297
Caribbean 318, 340, 349, 427
see also West Indies
Caribs 317, *451*
Carloman 186
Carmel, Mount 267
Carmelites *266*, 267
Carnac 30–31, *31*
Carnarvon, Earl of 5
Carolina 482
Caroline Islands 697
Carolingian empire 186, 206
Carothers, Wallace 687
"Carpet-baggers" 585
Carrhae, battle of (53 B.C.) 112
Carroll, Lewis 584
Cars 589, *589*, 609, 613, 660, *661*
Carson, Rachel 744
Carter, Howard 3, **5**, *5*, 664
Carthage 67, 73, 82, 94

White Lotus rebellion
479, 503, 531
takes control of Tibet 491
18th century trade **502–503**
Christian missionaries
banned 525
invades Nepal 526
tea *549*
Boxer Rebellion 559, *561*, **622–623**
Opium wars 559, 565, **568–569**, 579, 581, 583
war with France 559
war with Japan 559, 579
paintings *566*
Taiping rebellion *568*, 569, 572
first railroad 611
"Hundred Days of Reform" 620, 622
Civil War 639, 640, 672–673, 682, 687, 710, 716, 734
communism 639, *641*, 663, 667, 672–673, 675, **716, 734–735**
Long March 639, **672–673**, 681
Japanese invasion of Manchuria **686–687**
Chinese-Japanese War **687**, *687*, 688, 703
World War II **696–697**
People's Republic created 714
Cultural Revolution 719, 720, 729, 735
war with India 719, 726
earthquakes 737
birth control *743*
Tiananmen Square massacre 719, *735*, 742, *742*
dynasties 746
Chintz *485*
Chios 551
Chippewas *391*
Chisholm, Shirley 730
Chivalry 244–245, 314
Chocolate 355
Cholera 606
Chongqing 687
Chou dynast *see* Zhou dynasty
Chouart, Medard *468*
Christ *see* Jesus Christ
Christian IV, King of Denmark 423
Christian Science Church 601
Christianity:
in Roman empire 78, 80, 124, 125, *125*, 129, 136
in Africa 102
spread of **128–129**
Nicene Creed 136
in Armenia 151
split between Churches of Rome and Constantinople 152
monasteries **156, 166–169**
St. Patrick converts Irish 156
Dark Ages 160
Orthodox Church 163, 167
Picts converted to 168
in Britain 168, 174, **203**
Celtic Church 178
persecution of Jews 178–179

Bulgars converted 184
Copts 184, 186
in Russia 185
Prester John 192, 283
Magyars convert to 200, *201*
501–1100 A.D. 204
Crusades 237, 242–243, 284
in Ethiopia **265**
missionaries 274, 319, 392, *393*, 402–403, *403*, 417, *445*, 596
pilgrimages 284
Great Schism **296–297**, 299, 302, 304, 307
indulgences 296
massacres in Japan 430
Boxer Rebellion 622, *623*
see also Protestants; Roman Catholic Church
Chronometers 534
Chrysler Building, New York *640*, 655, 675
Chrysoloras, Manuel 330
Chu Yuen-Chang 294, 295
Church of England 350, 351, 363, 371, 376
Church of Jesus Christ of Latter-day Saints 525
Church of Scotland 376
Churches *253*, *285*, *364*
Churchill, Sir Winston *1*, 694, **695**, *695*, 700, 701, 702, 722
Cicero 115
Cimmarians 70
Cincinnati observatory 590
Cinema 566, 567, *602*, 616, 660, 672, 676, 677
Cistercians 167, 232
Citeaux 232
Cities, ancient **22–23**
see also individual cities
Civil rights movement 718, 722, 726, 729, 737
Civil Service, China **294**
Cixi, Empress Dowager of China 620, **622**
Clairvaux Abbey 242
Clarence, George, Duke of 329, 336
Clark, William 536
Class system 138, *202*, 676
Claude Lorraine 404
Claudius, Appius 94
Claudius I, Emperor 121
Claudius II, Emperor 135
Clausewitz, Karl von *554*
Clay tablets 28, 49, *60*
Cleisthenes 74
Clement IV, Pope 270
Clement V, Pope 281, 296
Clement VI, Pope 288
Clement VII, Pope 296, *358*, 361
Clement VIII, Pope 393
Clement XI, Pope 466
Cleopatra II, Queen of Egypt 104
Cleopatra VII, Queen of Egypt 94, **95**, *95*, 115, 118, 155
Cliff Palace, Mesa Verde *183*
Clifton Suspension Bridge *574*
Climate, Ice Age 12–13
Clocks:
Chinese *211*

candle *212*
watches 350, 373
pendulum clocks *452*
minute hands 453
cuckoo clocks 502
chronometers *534*
atomic clocks 690
Cloisonné enamel *405*
Clontarf, battle of (1014) 218, 250
Clothes:
ancient Egyptian *36*
Minoan *36*
Etruscan *37*
Sumerian *37*
Chinese 116
Roman *117*
501–1100 A.D. 196, *196*
Viking *217*
Japanese 276, *516*
Middle Ages 277, *301*
in the Renaissance 357, *357*
Elizabethan *375*
17th century 434, *434*
19th century *602*, 603
jeans *616*
20th century 677, *677*, *691*
Clovis, King of the Franks 151, 152, 156, 162, 186
Cluniac order 167, 203
Cluny Abbey 167, 203
Cooperative movement 569
Coal mining 491, 541, 543, *543*, *618*
Coalbrookdale *491*, *492*, 519
Coblenz, Treaty (1338) of 288
Coca-Cola 707
Cochin-China 583, 604
Cod, Cape 398, 409, 417
Codron, King of Athens 55
Coffee 353, *429*, *429*, 450, 494, 527
Coffee houses *400*, *420*, 421, 429, 437, 438, 455, 494
Coins:
in ancient world 60, *60*, 61, **83**, *83*
Chinese 149
Viking 228
Florence *288*
Mogul *469*
Colbert, Jean 436, *439*
Cold War 720, *720*, **722–723**, 724
Coleridge, Samuel Taylor 485
Coligny, Admiral Gaspard de 378–379
Colla tribe 322, 327
Collins, Michael 649, 656, *662*, *667*
Cologne 179, 216, 257, 288
Cologne, Confederation of 295
Colombia 318, 346, 537, 626
Colombo 353
Colonialism:
European 557
"scramble for Africa" **598–599**
British empire **610–611**
Colosseum, Rome *1*, 93, 117, *127*
Colossi of Memnon 42
Colt, Samuel *633*
Colt revolvers *554*, *633*
Columba, St 168, 169
Columbus, Christopher 317, 318, *320*, 329, *329*,

340, *340*, *341*, *342*, 346, *348*, 350, 408, 429, 450
Columns, architecture *88*
Combine harvesters *669*
COMECON 714, 729, *729*
Comédie Française 456
Cominform 709
Commedia dell'arte 435
Committee of Public Safety 522, 523, 532
Commodus, Emperor 129
Common Market *see* European Economic Community
Common markets 728–729
Commonwealth (Cromwell) 431, 442
Commonwealth of Nations 675, 679, 707, **714–715**, 730
Communications:
in the ancient world **28–29**
in the classical world **100–101**
501–1100 A.D. **180–181**
Middle Ages **260–261**
Renaissance **342–343**
17th century **420–421**
18th century **500–501**
19th century **588–589**
20th century **660–661**, 740
Communism:
founders of *619*
in Eastern Europe 638, 701
in China 639, *641*, 663, 667, 672–673, 675, **716, 734–735**
Russian Revolution *651*, 652
Spartakist uprising 656
in Greece 705
Cold War 720, **722–723**, 724
McCarthyism 722
Warsaw Pact 722
collapse in Eastern Europe 718, **738–739**, 744
Comnenian empire 322
Compasses 123, 133, *213*, 257, 339, *339*, 344
Computers 3, 551, *613*, 690, *691*, 703, 721, 738, *738*, 740
Comyn, John 275
Concentration camps 679, 681, **694**, *694*
Concorde (aircraft) 730, *730*, *741*
Concrete, discovery of 92
Confederacy 558, *582–583*, *583*
Confucianism 124
Confucius 11, **73**, *73*, 99, 107, 120, 525
Congo 598–599, 630
see also Zaire
Congo River 339, 340, 398, 433
Congress (U.S.) 670, 710
Connaught 250
Connecticut 398, 474, 476, 502
Connolly, James 648, **649**, *649*
Conquistadores **362–363**, 366–367
Conrad II, Holy Roman Emperor 218
Conrad III, Holy Roman Emperor 245

trade 257
Hanseatic League 267, **288–289**
Reformation 354–355, 358, 371
clothes 357
Thirty Years' War 397, 414–415, **416–417**, 419, 424, 435
League of Augsburg 458, 463, 466
War of the Spanish Succession 471
cuckoo clocks 502
Second empire 593
nationalism 571
Confederation dissolved 586
socialism 590
North German Confederation **592–593**
League of Three Emperors 593
currency 596
"scramble for Africa" 598
Dual Alliance 601
African colonies 605
Triple Alliance 605, 636, 642
origins of World War I 623, 628, 636
World War I 642–645, 648, 651–652, 656–657
arms race 643
Spartakist uprising 656
aftermath of World War I 658–659, 663, 667, 672
hyperinflation 658
fascism 666
Hitler and the Nazis 675, 679, **680–681**
Third Reich 679
unemployment 679
Weimar Republic **680**
occupies Rhineland 682
Austrian Anschluss **688–689**
World War II 638, 692–696, *692*, 700–701
division into East and West 638
Berlin Airlift 710, 714
reunification 718, 739, 744
rulers 753
see also Prussia, Austria, Holy Roman Empire
Gershwin, George 647, 667
Gestapo *680*
Gettysburg, battle of (1863) 583, 584
Gettysburg Address 584
Ghana 158, *161*, 714, 718
see also Gold Coast
Ghana, kingdom of 192–193, 207, 217, 225, 229, 231, 264
Ghaznavid Turks 230
Ghazni 214
Ghent, Pacification of (1576) 386
Ghent, Treaty of (1814) 543
Ghettos 179
Ghidyas-ud-din Tughluk 283
Giacometti, Alberto *647*
Gibraltar 322, *470*, 474
Giffard, Henri 576
Gilbert, Humphrey 391
Gilbert, William 593
Gilbert Islands 697

Gilboa, battle of (1000 B.C.) 57
Gilgamesh 33, *47*
Girl Guides 630
Giza 21, 26, *27*, 33
Gladiators 117, *117*, *127*
Glasgow University 312
Glasses 293
Glass windows *413*
Glassware, Phoenician *57*
Glastonbury 209
Glencoe Massacre 459
Glendower, Owen 302, 304, 307
Globe Theatre, London *325*
Glorious Revolution 398, **458–459**
Goa 353, 376
Gobelins factory 436, *436*
God Save the Queen 506
Godfrey of Bouillon, King of Jerusalem 232
Gods and goddesses 44, 97, 204
Godunov, Boris 383, 393, 407, *407*
Godwin, Earl of Essex 222–223, 225
Goethe, Johann Wolfgang 485
Gogol, Nikolai 562
Gold:
El Dorado **367**
gold rushes 572, 583, 614, **616–617**, 631
in South Africa 609
Gold Coast 318, 339, 398, *400*, 427, **462**, 596
see also Ghana
Golden Gate Bridge, San Francisco *654*, 687
Golden Hind 374
Golden Horde 264, 272, 273, 299, 336, 382
Golden Horn 303, *303*
Golden Temple, Amritsar *444*
Goldmark, Peter 710
golf 616
Gone with the Wind 693
Good Hope, Cape of 307, 318, 338, 339, 340, 352, 398, 426–427, *428*, 439, 506, 531
Good Parliament 296
Goodpasture, Ernest 675
Goodyear, Charles 565
Gorbachev, Mikhail 718, 738–739, *741*, 744
Gordian, Emperor 131
Gordon, General 605, 609
Gordon Riots 519, *524*
Gospels 122, 126, *169*, *203*, 267
Gotamiputa Sri Satakani 126
Gothic architecture 252, 253, *253*
Gothic type 313
Goths 135, 143, 144, 146, 151
Government:
democracy 82, **83**
in the classical world **138–139**
501–1100 A.D. **220–221**
Middle Ages **300–301**
in the Renaissance **380–381**
17th century **460–461**
18th century **540–541**
1848 revolutions 570–571
19th century **618–619**

20th century **698–699**
Goya, Francisco 484, *540*
Gozo 31, 33
Grahame, Kenneth 630
Gramophones *612*
Granada *328*, 329, 340
Granada, Treaty of (1500) 346
Grand Alliance 482
Grand Canal (China) 170, *170*, 174, 181, *181*
Granson 332
Grant, Ulysses S. 582, *582*, 584, *585*
Grasso, Ella 734
Gratian, Emperor 143
Gravelines, battle of *374*
Graves, Robert 647
Great Britain *see* Britain
Great Depression (1930s) 646, 666, *669*, 676, **678–679**, 686
Great Exhibition, London (1851) 572, 575, *612*
Great Interregnum 267
Great Lakes 12, 501, 539
Great migrations 34–35
Great Mosque, Cordoba *173*
Great Northern War 398, **466–467**, 471, 473
Great Plague (1664–1665) 442, *443*, 446
Great Plains 614, 620–621
Great Plains Indians *380*, 390, *391*
Great Purge (USSR) 653
Great Pyramid, Giza 9, 10, 26, 33
Great Reform Bill (1832) 546
Great Schism 238, **296–297**, 299, 302, 304, 307
Great Stupa, Sanchi 97
Great Trek 562, 564, *564*
Great Wall of China 79, 93, 98, *98–99*, 171
Great War *see* World War I
Great Zimbabwe 195, *241*, **280–281**
El Greco 325
Greece 77, 80, **82–83**
historians 1, 7
migrations 35, 39
Minoan civilization **38–39**
Mycenaean culture **40–41**, 50
Arcadians 49
Dorian invasions 10, 55
Olympic games 64
warfare 68, *69*, 154, *154*
Trojan wars 69
government 70, 73, 74
tyrants 70
Dark Age **72**
sports *81*
city-states 67, 78, **84–85**
Persian wars 82
Peloponnesian wars 85
arts and crafts 86, 95
democracy 138, *139*
trade 148, *148*
legacy of the Greeks **88–89**
Spartan wars 89
Alexander the Great **90–91**, 90
architecture 92
travel 100, *101*
Macedonian wars 103
farming 109
influence on Rome 66, 115
theater *116*, 117

toys *116*
religion 124, *124*
science and technology *132–133*, 292
Goths attack 135
reconquers Cyprus 186
Ottoman Turks invade 302
influence on the Renaissance 317, 330
Venetians bombard Athens 458
independence from Ottoman empire 478, 551, **552**, 553
Balkan wars 634–635
Balkan Pact 681
monarchy restored 681
World War II 694
civil war 704, 705, *705*, 714
"Greek fire" *163*
Greek language 94
Green revolution *740*
Greenland 158, 201, 211, 217, 218, 407
Greenpeace 719, 744
Greenwich Observatory 450
Gregorian calendar 391, **396**, 510, 652
Gregory I the Great, Pope 171, 203
Gregory II, Pope 184
Gregory VII, St., Pope 211, *211*, 231
Gregory IX, Pope 263, 264
Gregory X, Pope 270
Gregory XI, Pope 295, 296
Gregory XII, Pope 304
Gregory XIII, Pope 384, 396
Gregory XV, Pope 417
Grenada 714, 738
Grenville, Richard 391
Grey, Lady Jane 371
Grimm brothers 539
Gropius, Walter 654
Guadalcanal, battle of (1942) 696
Guadalupe–Hidalgo, Treaty of (1848) 563
Guam 558, 620
Guangzhou (Canton) 568, 667, 688
Guatemala *93*, 135, 551, 737
Guericke, Otto von 438, *452*, 453
Guernica 683, 687, 713
Guiana 427
Guilds 257, *257*, 309
Guillotines *522*
Guiscard, Robert, Duke of Apulia 231
Guise family 376, 379
Gujarat 361, 384
Gujarat, battle of (1849) 572
Gulf War 744
Gunpowder 171, *213*, 217, 251, 314, *314*, 394, *417*
Gunpowder Plot *406*, 407
Guns *see* War and weapons
Gunthamund, King of the Vandals 152
Gupta dynasty 77, 79, **136–137**, 138, 140, 143, 151, 159, 167
Gurjaru-Prathi-Nara dynasty 186
Guru Nanak 319
Gustavus Adolphus, King of Sweden 398, 411, **414–415**, *416*, 417, 423, 424, *472*
Gustavus Vasa, King of Sweden 358

Gutenberg, Johannes 260, 261, 310, 312–313, *312–313*
Guyana 714
Gyges, King of Lydia 70

H

Hāfiz 247
Haakon the Great, King of Norway 214
Habeas Corpus 455, 461
Habsburg dynasty 370–371, 419, **422**, 423, 458, 470, 656
Hackney coaches 421
al-Hadi, Caliph 190
Hadrian, Emperor 126, 129, 141
Hadrian's Wall 93, 129, **141**
Hagar Qim 31
The Hague 623, 628, 633
Haile Selassie, Emperor of Ethiopia 265, 675, 718, 734
Hairstyles, 17th century *434*
Haiti *480*, 526
see also Santo Domingo
al-Hakim, Caliph 218
Hall, Charles Martin 609
Halley, Edmond 453, 474
Halley's comet 474, 553
Ham Nghi 604
Hamadan 74
Hamburg 288, 526
Hammamat, Wadi *42*
Hammurabi the Great, King of Babylon 40, **47**, 47
Hampshire 202
Hampton Court 334, *444*
Han dynasty 77, 79, 103, **120–123**, 129, 131
Handel, George Friderick 484, 504
Hanging Gardens of Babylon 71, *71*, 73
Hangzhou 233
Hankou 688
Hannibal 98, 103, *106–107*, 107
Hanoi 605
Hanover 466, 496
Hanover, Treaty of (1725) 494
Hanseatic League 267, **288–289**, 295, *308*, 309
Hara Castle *445*
Harald Hardrada, King of Norway 222, 223, 227, 234
Harappa 32, 33
Harding, Warren 659, **670–671**, *670*
Hardy, Thomas 596
Harem 380
Harfleur 304
Hargraves, Edward 616–617
Hargreaves, James *490*, 513
Harold I, King of England 222
Harold II, King of England 5, 223, *223*, 225, 227, 234
Harper's Ferry 581
Harrison, John *534*
"Harrying of the North" 227
Harsha, Emperor 174
Harthacanute, King of Denmark and England 222

Hartog, Captain 399
Harun al-Rashid, Caliph 190–191, *190*, 192
Harvard, John 427, 474
Harvard College *400*, **475**
Harvey, William 397, 423, 447, *453*
Hasan ibn al-Sabbah 232
Hastings, battle of (1066) *223*, *227*, *234*, *234*
Hathaway, Anne 375
Hatshepsut, Queen of Egypt 42, **54**, *54*, *55*
Hausa peoples 201, *462*, 478, 536
Havana 620
Hawaii:
first settlers 79, 126, 152
Tahitians migrate to 239, 257
Captain Cook killed in 512, 519
American missionaries 551
becomes part of U.S.A. 615, *615*, 620, 719, 725
World War II 639, 694, 696, 707
Hawkins, Sir John 374, 376, 379, 391
Hawthorne, Nathaniel 572
Hayam Wuruk 291
Hay-Pauncefort Treaty (1901) 623
Hayes, Rutherford B. 585, 599, 620
Hearths *197*
Hebrew calendar 27
Hebrew language 179
Hebrews 35, 50
Hegira 159, 174
Heijden, Jan van der 450
Heijden, Nicholas van der 450
Heinlein, Peter 373
Helen of Troy 40
Helicopters 682, *727*
Helios 125
Hellenistic period 77, 94
Helmets *235*
Hemingway, Ernest 670, 672, 722
Hengest 146
Henlein, Peter 350
Henrietta Maria, Queen 418, 424, 430
Henry, Joseph 553
Henry, Prince (son of Henry II) 251
Henry I, King of England *226*, 232, 238, 242, 245, 248
Henry I, King of France 222
Henry I the Fowler, King of Germany 207
Henry II, King of England 248–249, 250, 251, 464
Henry II, King of France 368, 375, 376, 378, 379
Henry III, Holy Roman Emperor 222
Henry III, King of England 263, 267, 270
Henry III, King of France 379, 384
Henry IV, Holy Roman Emperor 211, *211*, 225, 231
Henry IV, King of England 302
Henry IV (Henry of Navarre), King of France

378, **379**, 398, 408, 418
Henry V, Holy Roman Emperor 242, 245, 248
Henry V, King of England 304, *305*, 307
Henry VI, Holy Roman Emperor 238, 254, 257
Henry VI, King of England 304, 307, 310, 312, 316, *326*, *329*
Henry VII, Holy Roman Emperor 281
Henry VII, King of England 316, *316*, 339, 340, 344, 350
Henry VIII, King of England 318, 325, 329, 340–341, 349, **350–351**, *350*, 353, 355, 358, 361, 363, 366, 368, 377, *395*
Henry of Anjou 238
Henry of Guise 379, 391
Henry the Navigator, Prince of Portugal 304, **306–307**, *307*
Henry of Portugal, Cardinal 386
Heraclius, Emperor 174, 177
Heraldry *315*
Herzegovina 583
see also Bosnia-Hercegovina
Herculaneum *4*, *124*, 126
Hercules *130*
Herero people 626
Heretics *365*, *369*
Hereward the Wake 227, 231
Herman, Robert 710
Hermits 166
Herod the Great *110*, 111, 115, 118
Herod Agrippa, King of Judea 121
Herodotus 6, 7, 7, 88
Hertz, Heinrich *588*, 611
Herzl, Theodore 616
Hewett, John 529
Heyerdahl, Thor 709
Hideyoshi *321*, 391, 392, *392*, 393, *393*, 394
Hieroglyphics 6, 26, 27, 28, *28*
Highwaymen *256*, *501*, 502
high wheeler 589
Higley, John 502
Hilderic, King of the Vandals 162
Hillary, Edmund 722
Himalaya mountains 123
Himeji Castle *321*, *394*
Himiko 146
Hindenburg (airship) 660, *681*
Hindenburg, Paul von 679, 680, *680*, 681
Hindenburg Line 652
Hindu Kush 64, 96
Hinduism *97*, *103*
Vedas 57, 65
Gupta dynasty 136–137
decimal system 137
suttee **137**
persecuted in India 449
"thugs" *524*
Indian Mutiny 608–609
riots 704, 708
Hindustan *361*
Hipparchus 103
Hippocrates 85, *88*
Hiram of Tyre 56, 58

Hirohito, Emperor of Japan 639, 670
Hiroshima 639, 697, *697*, 703, *713*
Hispaniola 374
History:
definition 1
archaeology **2–3**, *2–3*
historians **6–7**
local history **8**
Hitler, Adolf 638, 659, 666, 667, 675, 677, 679, **680–681**, *681*, 682, 687, 688–689, *688–689*, 692–695, *698*, 701
Hitler Youth 693
Hittites 11, 39, 40, 42, **46**, 49, 50, 53
Ho Chi Minh 703, 704
Hobbema, Meindert 404
Hochelaga 363
Hojo clan 239, 254–255, 263, 286
Hokusai *484*, 559
Holbein, Hans 324, 325, 366
Holland *see* Netherlands
Holocaust 638, 694
Holy Land *see* Palestine
Holy League 344, 353, 395
Holy League of Linz 458
Holy Roman Empire 201, **206–207**, **371**
creation of 187
Treaty of Verdun 195
conflict with popes 210–211, 231, 288
kings of the Romans 215
Great Interregnum 267
civil war 283
Jews persecuted 291
and the Hanseatic League 295
and Italy *337*
war with Ottoman Turks 359, 361, 379, **384–385**, 443
Truce of Frankfurt 366
and the Habsburgs 370–371, 375
"Pragmatic Sanction" *482*
War of the Austrian Succession **482–483**
Napoleon conquers 536
emperors 752–753
Homer 3, 6, 10, 40, 41, 62, *62*, **72**, *72*
Homestead Act (1862) 614, 620
Homo erectus 14–15
Homo habilis 14
Homo sapiens 15
Honduras 135
Hong Kong:
tea trade *549*
Britain leases 568, 569
World War II 694, 696, 735
to be returned to China 719, 735, 741
Honorius, Emperor 144
Honorius III, Pope 263
Honorius IV, Pope 273
Hooghly River *528*
Hoover, Herbert Clark 675, 699
Hoover Dam 655, 682
Hopewell Indians 78, *80*, 86, 87, **134–135**, *134–135*, 149
Hopkins, Frederick 607
Hoplites 68, 72, *72*, 85

Ionic columns *88*
Iran:
oil reserves 630
World War II 694
Shah overthrown 719, 732, 738
Iran-Iraq War 719, 732, 738, 742
Kurds 736
see also Persian empire
Iraq *25*, 723
prehistoric 18
World War I 651
British mandate 658
World War II 694
oil *706*
Iran-Iraq War 719, 732, 738, 742
invades Kuwait 719, 733, 744
Kurds 736
Gulf War 744
see also Mesopotamia
Ireland:
St. Patrick converts to Christianity 146, **156**, *156*
Vikings in 195, 217, 218, 229, 250
High Kings **250–251**
Richard II's expedition against 302
Catholic Church 354
Earl of Tyrone's rebellions 379, 393
Protestants massacred in Ulster 430
Cromwell invades 437
James II lands in 459, 463
English rule **464–465**
Vinegar Hill rebellion 532
Act of Union (1801) 536
Home Rule issue 551, 558, 601, 609, 615, 642, 648, 659
famine 558, 569, 595, **600–601**
Easter Rising 638, **648–649**
Irish Free State established 638, 662, 663
civil war 649, 662, *663*, 664, 667
becomes a republic 656, **662–663**
leaves Commonwealth 714, 715
see also Northern Ireland
Irene, Empress 190, 192
Irish Citizen Army 649
Irish Land League 601
Irish Republican Army (IRA) 649, 656, 718, 730, 734, 738
Irish Republican Brotherhood 581, 648
Irish Sea 23
Irish Volunteers 648–649
Iron Age 46, 52, *53*, 59, 102
Iron Curtain 722
Iron lung *684*
Iron and steel 535
China *98*
Nok culture 102, *102*
tools 188
weapons 234
Darby's coke furnace 482
Industrial Revolution *491*
blast furnaces 506
steel-making *613*

Ironing boards *196*
Iroquois tribe *391*
Irrigation 19, *19*, *98*
Isaac II, Emperor 254
Isabella I, Queen of Spain **328–329**, *328*, 331, 336, 340
Isabella II, Queen of Spain 586
Isabella of France (wife of Edward II) 238, 286
Isabelle of France (wife of Richard II) 286, 302
Isandhlwana, battle of (1879) 564, 601
Isfahan 231, *324*, *346*, 347, *347*
Ishtar *44*, 70
Isin 47
Islam and Muslims:
Prophet Muhammad 168, 177, 204
foundation of Islam 157, **174–175**
arts and crafts 164, *164*, 165
symbol of *174*
spread of 158, 159, 160, *161*, **176–177**, 182, 184, 204
Umayyad dynasty 178, 186
Jews in 179
Abbasid dynasty 186, **190–191**
Fatimid dynasty 203
Druse sect 218
government 220
Crusades 232, 284
in Mali empire 264–265
science and technology *292*
Koran *300*
slavery *309*
Shiites 346, 364
Sunnis 364
in India 360–361
in Africa *462*, 560, 597
Wahhabism 524, 525
Indian Mutiny 608–609
riots in India 704, 708
militant fundamentalists 720
tensions between Shiites and Sunnis 733
Islamic Law 220, 300
Isle of Man 217
Isle of Wight 202, 431
Ismail I, Shah 346
Israel:
division into Israel and Judah 11
revolt against Philistines 57
see also Palestine
Israel, State of:
creation of 639, 640, **710–711**
War of Independence 639
wars with Arabs 711, 714, 729, 732–733, *732*, 734
Suez Crisis 733
invades Lebanon 719
peace treaty with Egypt 719, 738
Israelites 10, 40, 49, 50
Issus, battle of (333 B.C.) 90
Istanbul 358, *412*, 414, 665
see also Constantinople
Italy:
Villanova culture 57

foundation of Rome 64
Etruscans 82, 89, 94
Roman empire 77, **104–105**, 110, 118–119, **126–127**
trade 148, 256
Huns invade 143–145, 151
Ostrogoth kingdom 156
in Byzantine empire 162
monasteries 167
Lombards 168, 186
Arabs driven out of 201
Louis IV invades 286
government 300
city-states 331
Medici family 304, 329
Renaissance 330, **336–337**
France renounces claim to 361
France invades 366
plague 384
Commedia dell'arte 435
Italian-Turkish War 558, 635
unification 558, 583, **590–591**
nationalism 571
"scramble for Africa" 598
Triple Alliance 605, 636, 642
invades Ethiopia 609, 611, 616, 638, *666*, 681, 682
Fascism 638, 656, 664, 666–667, *667*, 670, 696, 701, 704
World War I 645, 658
World War II 692, 693, 694–695
after World War II **704**
presidents and prime ministers 757
Ivan III the Great, Grand Prince of Muscovy 318, 322, 331, 336, **382**, *382*, 383
Ivan IV the Terrible, Tsar 363, 368, 379, 381, **382–383**, *382*, 386, 391
Ivan V, Tsar 456
Ivory *494*, 532, *596*
Ivory Coast 615
Izmir 331, 664
Iznik pottery *384*

J

Jackson, Andrew **538**, *538*, 539
Jackson, Michael 743, *743*
Jacob 50
Jacobins *522*, *523*
Jacobites 477, 478, **486–487**, 488, *506*
Jacquard, Joseph-Marie *534*
Jacquerie 299
Jade *37*, *123*
Jahangir, Emperor of India 399, 407, 411, *435*, 440
Jainism 169
Jamaica 438, 450, 465, *544*, 584, 714
James I, King of England (James VI of Scotland) 374, 377, 383, 398, 402, 406–407, *406*, 411, *411*, *459*, *460*, 486
James I, King of Scotland 304

James I the Conqueror, King of Aragon 263
James II, King of England 442, 455, 458, 463, *464*, 465, 471, 486
James II, King of Scotland 312
James III, King of Scotland 312
James IV, King of Scotland 340, 346, 353, 395, 406
James V, King of Scotland 353, 368, 377
James VI, King of Scotland *see* James I, King of England
James, Henry 601
James Baines (American clipper) 625
Jameson Raid 565, 616
Jamestown 407, 408, 414, *460*
Janissaries *241*, *302*, 303
Janssen, Hans 393
Janssen, Zacharias 393
Jansz, Willem 399, 407
Japan:
Jomon culture 11, 39
Yamato period 79
arts and crafts 86
clothes *116*, *276*, *516*
Buddhism 144, 159, 168, 171, 204, *365*, *393*
499 B.C.–A.D. 500 **146–147**
Chinese influences 160, 178
loses Korea 168
constitution 174
Taikwa reforms 178
Fujiwara period **198–199**, 214
civil wars 209, 251, 286, 317, *321*, 326, **392**
emperors 220
Hojo clan 239, 263, 286
shoguns and samurai 240, **254–255**, 286, 314, *314*
Kamakura period 254
Mongols invade 267, 270, 273
Nō theater 283, *283*
Zen Buddhism *284*
Portuguese explorers 317, 319, 368, 392
invades Korea 319
Christian missionaries 319, 364, 365, 371, 392, 402–403, *403*, 417, 445
Kabuki theater 325, *405*
tea ceremony **393**
isolation **402–403**
Dutch traders *403*, 411
Christians massacred 430
Shimbara uprising 430
Sumo wrestling *435*
woodblock printing 484, *484*
famine 498, 519
Tokugawa shoguns **402–403**, 514
public baths *517*
ends isolation 531
Meiji period 559, **578–579**, 586, 611, *618*
Satsuma revolt 559, 599
wars with China 559, 579, **687**, *687*, 688, 703
Russo-Japanese War 559, 579, 626, 628, 629, *629*
annexes Korea 630
occupies Manchuria 639,

Louis XVI, King of France 478, 520, 522–523, 526, 529
Louis XVIII, King of France 542, 543, 545, 553
Louis the German 195
Louis the Pious, Emperor of the Franks 192, 195
Louis Napoleon *see* Napoleon III, Emperor
Louis-Philippe, King of France 553
Louisiana 411, 488
Louisiana Purchase 478, 536, 556
Low Countries:
trade 257, 308
see also Belgium; Netherlands
Loyola, Ignatius 363, 365, 366, **368–369**, *369*
Lübeck 288
Lübeck, Treaty of (1629) 423
Lublin, Union of 383
Lucknow 581, *608*
Lucullus 110
Luddites 539, *546*, 547
Lufthansa *661*
Luftwaffe 694, 695
Lui Pang, Emperor of China 103
Lulach, King of Scotland 225
Lumière brothers *602*, 616
Luoyang 131
Lupaca tribe 322, 327
Lusitania (British liner) 645
Luther, Martin 318, 350, **354–355**, *354*, 358, *365*
Lutherans 355
Lützen, battle of (1632) 415, 417, 424
Luxembourg 386–387, 694
Luxor 42, 46
Lydia 74
Lyon, Synod of 264
Lyons 553
Lysander of Sparta 82, 85

M

Ma Yuan, Emperor of China 121
Macao 353, 375, 393, *503*
MacArthur, General *697*
Macartney, Lord *503*
Macbeth, King of Scotland 195, *195*, 222, 225
Maccabeus, Judas 104, 110
Maccabeus, Simon 107
McCarthy, Senator Joe 722
McCormick, Cyrus 553, *594*
Macdonald, Flora 487, 506
Macdonald clan 459
McDonald's *739*
Macedonia 89, 90, 94, 295, 634–635
Macedonian wars 98, 103, 104
Machiavelli, Niccolo 381
Machine guns 488, 633, *713*
Machinery, farming *594–595*
Machu Picchu 327
MacIndoe, Sir Alexander 684
Mackenzie, William Lyon 586, *586*
McKinley, William 623
Mackintosh, Charles 535
MacNeish, Richard 3
Macon 182

Madagascar 398, 605, 616
Madeira 307, 353
Madras 425, *425*, 430
Madrid 376, 683, 693
Maga dynasty 192
Magadha 136
Magazines 588
Magdeburg 424
Magellan, Ferdinand 319, **340**, *340*, 341, *341*, 355, 358
Magenta, battle of (1859) 581
Magna Carta 238, **262–263**, 301
Magnus the Good, King of Denmark 222
Magyars 158, **200**, 203, 207
Mahabharata 97
Mahdists 558, 601, 609, 610, 616, 620
Mahmud, Shah of Afghanistan 494
Mahmud of Ghazni 214, 218
Maine (France) 248
Maine (U.S.A.) 218, 551
Mainz 310, 312
Maipú, battle of *536*
Majuba Hill, battle of (1881) 601
Makuria Kingdom 158
Malabar coast 350
Malacca 353, 426
Malaria *606*, 620
Malawi 714, 718, 729
Malaya 604, 694, 696, 710
Malaysia 159, 595, 714, 719, 726
Malcolm I, King of Scotland 209
Malcolm II, King of the Scots 194–195
Malcolm III, King of Scotland 195, 225, 232
Malcolm IV "The Maiden", King of Scotland 248
Maldives 714
Maldon, battle of (991) 214
Mali empire 193, 237, 238, 240, **264–265**, 318, 322, 344, *598*
Malik Shah 230, 231
Malory, Sir Thomas 339
Malplaquet, battle of (1709) 471
Malta 31, 33, 57, 198, 361, 379, 384–385, 714
Maltese Cross 385, *385*
Malthus, Thomas 508
Mama Ocllo 278
Mameluke dynasty 355, 506–507
Mamun the Great, Caliph 192
Manasseh, King of Judah 67
Manaus 575
Manchester 545, *546*, 547
Manchu dynasty 622–623
Manchukuo 679, 686
Manchuria 120, 623, 629, 639, 675, 679, **686–687**
Manchus 393, 399, 414, 427, **432–433**, 466
Manco Capac 238, 263, 278
Mandates, League of Nations **658**
Mande people *598*
Mandela, Nelson 718, 744, *744*
Mandingo empire 344

Manet, Edouard 584
Manhattan Island 398, 411, 427
Manhattan project 713
Manila 696
Manitoba *587*
Mann, Thomas 623, 667
Mansa Musa, King of Mali 238, 264, *264*, 281, 283
al-Mansur 159, 190
Mantua 336
Manuel Comnenus, Emperor 239, 248
Manuscripts *227*, *267*, 277
Manzikert, battle of (1071) 230, 231, 234
Mao Zedong 639, **672–673**, *672*, 681, 687, 714, 716, *716*, 719, 734–735, *734*, 737
Maoris *161*, **236**, 454, *481*, 513
woodcarvings *164*
migration to New Zealand 239, 279
clashes with Europeans *512*, 559, *561*, 569, **572–573**
Maps:
Arab *212*
Renaissance *329*, *389*
Henricus Martellus *340*
Waldeseemuller's world map 350
Mercator 366
Mar, Earl of *486*, 487
Marathas 441, 479, 494, *495*, 497, 515, 519, 536, 547
Marathon, battle of (490 B.C.) 82, 83, 100, 155
Marcellus 98
Marchfeld, battle of (1278) 273
Marconi, Guglielmo *589*, 623
Margaret, Queen of Scotland (Maid of Norway) 274, 275
Margaret, St., Queen of Scotland 195
Margaret of Anjou 329
Margaret of Valois 379
Margaret of York 326
Margaret Tudor 406
Margarine 590
Marggra, Andreas 506
Mari 39, 47
Maria Theresa, Empress of Austria 482, **483**, *483*, 506
Maria Theresa of Spain 437
Mariana Islands 697
Marie Antoinette, Queen of France 522–523, *522*, 529
Marie de Medici 379, **418**, *418*
Marignano, battle of (1515) 353
Marius, Gaius 107
Marjdabik, battle of (1516) 353
Mark, St. *203*
Markets *109*, 256, 308, *308*
Marlborough, John Churchill, 1st Duke of 413, **470–471**, **471**, 474
Marne, 1st battle of (1914) 642
Marne, 2nd battle of (1918) 652
Maroons *544*

Marquesas Islands 239, 279
Marquette, Father Jacques *410*, 411, 450
Marrakesh 225
Mars (planet) 725, 733
Marseille 57
Marsh Arabs *25*
Marshall, George 709
Marshall Islands 697
Marshall Plan 638, 701, 709, 710
Marston Moor, battle of (1644) 433
Martel, Charles, King of the Franks 158, 184, 186, 234
Martellus, Henricus *340*
Martin IV, Pope 273
Martin V, Pope 297, 307
Martinique 427
Marx, Karl 558, 571, 586, *619*, **628**, *628*
Marxism 590, 628
Mary, Queen of Scots 368, 375, 376, *376*, **377**, *377*, 379, 383, 391
Mary, Virgin 445
Mary (wife of Louis XII) 353
Mary I, Queen of England (Mary Tudor) 351, 369, 371, 375, 376, 464
Mary II, Queen of England 443, 455, **458–459**, *458–459*, 463, 465
Mary of Burgundy 332
Mary of Guise 377
Mary Rose **351**, *351*, 356, *366*
Maryland 424, 437, *475*, 476, 513
Masada *111*, 122
Masina 515
Maskelyne, Neville 513
Masks *116*
Masolino 332
Mason-Dixon line 513
Massachusetts 398, 417, 423, 469, 476, 515
Massachusetts Bay 474
Massacre of St. Brice's day (1002) 217
Massagetae tribe 74
Massawa 609
Massice, battle of (244 B.C.) 131
Massys, Quentin *388*
Mastabas 27, *27*
Masts, battle of the (655) 178
al-Masudi 203
Masurian Lakes, battle of (1914) 642
Matabele War 558, 615
Matabeleland 558, 565
Matchlock guns 314, *416*, *473*
Mathematics:
Babylonian 47
ancient Greece 88
decimal system **137**
Mayan 151
Hindu-Arabic numerals 213, 258
algebra 293
in the Renaissance *372*
decimal point 411
17th century 452
Matilda, Empress 242, 245, 248
Matisse, Henri 628
Mato Grosso *744*
Matteotti, Giacomo 667
Matthias, Holy Roman Emperor 411

first playhouse 485
Federal Capital of U.S.A. 520
population 551
Statue of Liberty *574*, 609
chain stores 625
skyscrapers *640*, *655*, *671*
UN headquarters 703
New York Stock Exchange 678
New York Sun 553
New Zealand:
  Polynesians settle in 159
  Maoris *161*, **236**, 239, 279
  first white explorers 399, 454
  Captain Cook visits *481*, 512–513
  whaling *548*
  in British empire 557, 565, 628
  constitution 559, 576
  Dominion founded 559
  European colonization *561*, 569, **572–573**
  gold rush 583
  women's rights 615, 627
  World War I 644, 645
  in the Commonwealth 714, 715
  independence 715, *715*
  ANZUS alliance 719, 722
  bans nuclear weapons 741
  prime ministers 758
Newcastle, "Mad Madge", Duchess of 435
Newcastle-upon-Tyne 264
Newcomen, Thomas 482, *490*
Newfoundland 158, 218, 344, 374, 391, 417
Newspapers 408, 421, *421*
Newton, Sir Isaac 397, 434, 446, 447, *447*, 449, **452**, 453, 456, 458, 466, 474
Niagara Falls 455
Nicaea, Council of (787) 190
Nicaragua 346, 628, 638, 670, 718, 723, 737, 738
Nice 583, *591*
Nicene Creed 136
Nicephorus, Emperor *185*
Nicholas I, Tsar 579
Nicholas II, Tsar 558, 616, 623, **628**, *628*, 629, *650*, 651, 652
Nicholas III, Pope 273
Nicholas IV, Pope 274
Nicopolis 302
Nicot, Jean 376
Niépce, Joseph 551
Niger River 264, 531, *598*
Nigeria:
  kingdom of Daura 201
  Britain occupies Lagos 572
  in the Commonwealth 714
  Biafran war 718, 729, 730, 731, 733
  independence 718, 726
  see also Benin; Dahomey; Nok culture
"Night of the Long Knives" (1934) 681
Nightingale, Florence 576, *576*, 579, 607
Nijinsky, Vaslav *646*
Nijmegen, Treaty of (1678) 455
Nile River 9, 18, *20*, 24, 26, 149

Nimes *92*
Niña (Columbus's ship) *341*
Nineveh 49, 67, 177
Nixon, Richard M. 718, 734
No Man's Land 644
Nō theater 239, 283, *283*
Noah's Ark 6, 24, 25
Nobel, Alfred 613, *633*
Nobel Prizes *633*, 685, *691*, 729
Nobunaga, Oda 392, *392*
Nogaret, Guillaume de 281
Nok culture 58, 78, *80*, 82, 85, *87*, 102, 133
Nola, battle of (215 B.C.) 98
Nomads *35*, *380*
Nordlingen, battle of (1634) 424
Norman Conquest 5, 158, 188
Normandy 158, 203, 214, 217, 226, 238, 248, 258, 304, 695, 701
Normans 226–227
  architecture *172*, 173
  in England 221, *221*, 223, *234*
  in Sicily 231
  in Ireland 251
North Africa:
  Vandal kingdom 146, 151, 152, 162, 167, 182
  in Byzantine empire 158, 162
  Islamic empire 160, 182
  Fatimid dynasty 203, 207
  Almoravid dynasty 225
  Almohades 238, 248
  Portuguese conquests 329
  and the Ottoman empire 371, 384
  World War II 694, 696
  see also individual countries
North America:
  ancient history 27, 80
  great migrations 34
  Hopewell Indians 78
  farming 109, 188, 428
  Temple Mound culture 158
  first towns 160, **182–183**
  Vikings in 217, 218, 254
  exploration of 341, 368, 450
  European settlers, 379, 391, 397, *397*, 400, *400*, **408–411**, **474–476**
  religion *444*
  government *460*
  trade 468
  wars between British and French **498–499**, 510
  British taxes 513
  Mason-Dixon line 513
  American Revolution 515, **518–519**
  Boston Tea Party 515, *519*
  Continental Congress 515
  railroads 557
  settlement of 560
  in the 19th century **614–615**
  see also Canada; Mexico; Native North Americans; United States of America
North Atlantic Treaty Organization (NATO) 638, 714, 722, 723, 738
North Carolina 465, 476, 556
North German

Confederation 558, 586, 592–593
North Pole 12, 630
North Sea 12, 448, 729, *729*
Northwest Frontier *609*
Northwest Territories (Canada) 587
Northampton, battle of (1460) 312
Northern Ireland (Ulster):
  Protestant Plantation of Ulster 411, 464–465
  Protestants massacred 430
  creation of 659, 662, 663, *663*
  fighting between Catholics and Protestants 730, 733
  IRA hunger strikes 738
  see also Britain
Northern Song dynasty *232*
Northumbria 177, 178, 190, 198, 202, *203*, 207, 209, 218, 225
Norway:
  skiing 34
  Vikings *157*
  Union of Kalmar 302
  Protestant faith *354*
  independence 628
  World War II 693, 694
Notre Dame, Paris 253
Nova Scotia 417
Novara, battle of (1513) 353
Novella, Maria di 279
Novgorod 185, 198, 218, 264, **288**, *288*, 336, 382, 383
Noyon, Treaty of (1516) 353
Nubia 10, 24, 58, *59*, 64
Nuclear power 718, 741, 744–745, *745*
Nuclear weapons 718, 719, 722–723, *723*, 734, 741, 742
  see also Atomic bombs
Numa Pompilius, King of Rome 67
Numbers:
  Babylonian 47
  decimal system **137**
  Arabic 258, 293
Numidia 107
Numitor, King 66
Nuns 166–168, **169**, 266, *266*
Nur Jahan, Empress *435*, 440
Nuremberg, Peace of (1532) 363
Nuremberg Laws 681
Nuremberg rallies *680*, *687*
Nuremberg war trials 638, 700, 703
Nylon 687, 690, *691*

O

Oates, Titus 455
Oba Ewuare 238
Obelisks, Axum 102, *103*
O'Casey, Sean 667
Oceania 76, 454, **512–513**
O'Connell, Daniel 601, *601*
Octavia 118
Octavian *see* Augustus, Emperor
October Revolution (1917) 652
Odessa 526

Odin 204, *205*, 217
Odoacer 152
Odyssey (Homer) 62, *62*, 72
Oersted, Hans Christian 547
Offa, King of England 186, 190, 192, *186*, 202
Offa's Dyke 186
Oglethorpe, James 498
Ogodai Khan 264, 270–271
Ohio *78*, *80*
Ohio valley 135, 498, 510
Oil:
  19th century industry 612, 613
  in Middle East *706*
  price rises 719, 728, 734
  in North Sea 729, *729*
  Iraq invades Kuwait 733
  pollution *745*
Oklahoma *556*, 558, 611
Olaf I Tryggvason, King of Norway 214, 217
Olaf II, King of Norway 218, 222
Olaf Skutkonung, King of Sweden 214
"Old Man of the Mountain" 232
Old Pretender *see* Stuart, James
Old Testament 50
Olmecs 10, 16, *16*, *21*, 62–63, *63*
Olympia 88
Olympic Games 9, 10, 64, *64*, 88, *89*, 143, 558, 603, 616, 667, 682, *698*, 733
Oman 506
Omar I, Caliph 177
Omar Khayyam 245
Omdurman, battle of (1898) 620
Oñate, Juan de 475
Opera *484*, 566, *575*
Opium 502, *503*
Opium wars 559, 565, **568–569**, 579, 581, 583
Oracle bones 43
Oral history 6, 8
Orange Free State 564–565, 586, 599, 623
Oranges *508*
Oranienburg 679
Order of the Garter 291
Oregon Treaty (1846) 571
Organization for African Unity (OAU) 730
Organization for Economic Cooperation and Development (OECD) 729, *729*
Organization of Petroleum Exporting Countries (OPEC) 718, 719, 726, 728, 734
Orkhan I, Sultan 239, 286
Orkney Islands 30, *30*, 31, 34, 39, *194*
Orleans, siege of (1428–1429) 304, 307
Ormonde, James Butler, Duke of 465
Ormuz *346*, 353
Orthodox Church 163, 167, *185*, 198, 201, 214, 225, 382
Orwell, George 703, 714
Oseberg ship *165*
Osei Tutu 398, 462, 463
Osman I, Sultan 279, 302
Ostrogoths 143, 144, *145*, 151, 152, 156, 167

Oswald, King of Northumbria 202
Oswy, King of Northumbria 178, 202
Othman, Caliph 177, 178
Otho, Emperor 122
Otis, Elisha Graves 579
Otluk-beli, battle of (1472) 331
Ottakar I, King of Bohemia 257
Ottakar of Bohemia 273
Otto I, Emperor of Germany 6, 158, 200, 206–207, *207*, 209, 211
Otto I, King of Greece *552*
Otto II, Holy Roman Emperor 211
Otto IV, Holy Roman Emperor 257, 258
Otto, Nikolaus 599, 613
Ottoman empire:
　captures Constantinople 142, 285
　foundation of 231, 237, 239, 279, 286
　Janissaries *241*
　army crosses into Europe 288
　spread of 299, 302, 312, 322, 329, 332, 336, 355, 358, 363, 368, 371, 380
　fall of Constantinople **302–303**, 312, 315
　Tamerlane overruns 302
　civil war 304
　besieges Vienna 318
　war with Venice 319, 322, 331, 433, 438, 449
　arts and crafts 324
　Venice pays tribute to 336
　wars with Persia 346, 353, 359, 399, 402, 494, 498
　war with Egypt 353, 355
　golden age **358–359**
　war with Hungary 363, 371
　truce with Holy Roman Empire 379
　tries to gain control of Mediterranean 383, **384–385**
　in North Africa 384
　makes peace with Safavid empire 393
　war with Austria 393, 455, 456, 465, 466
　conquers Baghdad 430
　war with Holy Roman Empire 443
　war with Poland 450, 455
　decline of 455
　war with Russia 455, 456, 482
　reforms 529
　Greek War of Independence 551, **552**, 553
　weapons *555*
　collapse of 557, 639, 640, 659, **664–665**
　Italian-Turkish War 558
　Russo-Turkish War 558
　war with Syria 565
　Crimean War **576–577**
　Balkan wars **634–635**
　see also Turkey
Ouchy, Treaty of (1912) 635
Oudenarde, battle of (1708) 471, 482
Oudh 494, 579

Oughtred, William 424
Ovid 115
Owen, Wilfred 646
Owens, Jesse *698*
Oxen *101*, *188*, *299*
Oxford 413, 421, 433, 437
Oxford University 251, 299
Oyo empire 318, 398, 462
Ozone layer 719, 737, 742, 744, 745

P

Pachacuti, Sapa Inca *240*, 278, *278*, 310, 322, 326–327
Pacific Ocean:
　prehistory 11
　ancient history 80
　Polynesians **152–153**
　chronology 79, 159, 239, 319, 399, 479, 559, 639, 719
　exploration of **454, 512–513**
　first flights across 672
　World War II **696–697**
　Kon Tiki voyage 709
Pacific Treaty (1922) 664
Pacification of Dunse (1639) 430
Pagan 274
Paine, Thomas 505, *505*, 526
Paintings:
　cave 3, 10, *12*, *15*, 16, 18, 76
　wall *4*, *137*
　frescoes *17*, *331*
　rock *59*, *76*
　Roman *87*
　icons *185*
　Chinese *233*
　Middle Ages 246
　portraits *247*
　Renaissance *332*
　17th century 404
　18th century 484
　19th century 566, *566–567*
　20th century *646–647*
Pakistan:
　ancient history 21, 32–33, 64–65
　creation of 639, 640, 708, 709, *709*
　war with India 719, 733
　becomes Islamic republic 725
Palatinate 463
"The Pale" 251
Palenque *151*
Palestine 110–111
　Egypt conquers 42
　Israelites occupy 49
　Jews 50–51
　period of the Judges 50
　Romans conquer 112
　Arabs conquer 176
　Crusades 205, 232, 237, **242–243**, 248, 254, 258, 274, 315
　pilgrimages 242
　Balfour Declaration 639, 651, 710
　partition plan 639, 709, 710–711
　British mandate 658, 710–711
　Jewish homeland 659
　Jewish immigration 693, 710
　see also Israel
Palestine Liberation

Organization (PLO) 719, 732
Palestinians 711, *711*, 737, 742
Palladian architecture 493
Palmstruck, Johann 440
Pampa Indians *545*
Pan-African Conference 623
Pan-American congress 551
Pan Chao 121
Panama 537, 551, 626
Panama Canal 611, 623, 626, 638, 642, *706*
Panipat, battle of (1526) 361, 395
Panipat, battle of (1556) 375
Pankhurst, Emmeline 626–627
Pannonia 118, 146
Panormus 97
Pantheon, Rome 93
Pantomime *435*
Papacy see Popes
Papal States:
　foundation 186
　Holy Roman Empire and 273
　battle of Lepanto 385
　Piedmont Sardinia invades 583
　annexed by Cavour 590, 591
　see also Popes
Paper-making 122, 126, *132*, 133, 213, 248, 264, 292
Paper money (banknotes) *309*, 440, 469, *469*, 532, 548
Papin, Denis 455
Papineau, Louis 562, **586**, *586*
Papua New Guinea 714, 719, 734
Papyrus 28, 29
Paracelsus 361
Paraguay 536, 638, 679, 681
Paraguayan War 558, 584, 590
Parchment 49, *180*, *260*
Pardoners 296
Pare, Amboise *372*
Paris:
　under the Franks 162
　Capetian dynasty 214
　trade 256
　Black Death 291
　Hundred Years' War 310
　17th century architecture 412
　fiacres 421
　Fronde 436
　first restaurant 515
　smallpox plague 517
　Parlement 520
　French Revolution 522–523
　July Revolution *553*
　Second Republic *571*
　water mains *574*
　Eiffel Tower *575*
　Franco-Prussian War 590
　Commune 593
　World War II 694, 701
　student uprising 730
　Pompidou Center 737, *737*
Paris, Peace of (1763) 497, 513
Paris, Peace of (1783) 519
Paris, Treaty of (1856) 577, 579

Paris University 248, *248*
Parisot de la Valette, Jean 384, *384*
Park, Mungo 531
Parkman, Francis 6, *6*
Parlement of Paris 520
Parliament (Britain) *300*
　first 263, 270
　Model Parliament 279
　taxation 288
　Good Parliament 296
　"Reformation Parliament" 361
　execution of Charles I 400
　Gunpowder Plot 406, 407
　"Addled Parliament" 411
　Petition of Right 423, 461
　Long Parliament 430
　Short Parliament 430
　in 17th century 460
Parma, Duke of 386
Parnell, Charles 600–601, *601*
Parr, Catherine 350, 368
Parthenon, Athens 82, *93*, 458, 545, *545*
Parthians *81*, 112, **130–131**
Paschal II, Pope 242
Passchendaele, battle of (1917) 644, *644*, 651
Passion plays 424
Pasternak, Boris 725
Pasteur, Louis 558, 581, 606, *607*
Patay, battle of (1429) 304
Patchwork quilts *520*
Pathé News 660
Pathet Lao 734
Patricians 104, *104*
Patrick, St. 146, **156**, *156*
Paul, St 121, 122, 129
Paul I, Tsar 510
Paul II, Pope 322
Paul III, Pope 363, 366, 368
Paul IV, Pope 371, 375
Paul V, Pope 407
Pausanias 85
Pavia 168
Pavia, battle of (1525) 358
Pax Romana 126
Paxton, Joseph 575
Payens, Hugues de 242
Peacock Throne 502
Pearl Harbor 639, 671, 694, 696, *697*, 707
Pearse, Pádraig 648, 649
Peary, Robert 630
Peasants:
　farming 268
　clothes *276*
　peasants' revolts **298–299**, 301
　French **438**
　Russian *511*
Pedlars *286*
Pedro I, Emperor of Brazil 537
Pedro II, King of Aragon 257
Pedro the Cruel, King of Castile 291
Peel, Sir Robert 553, 600
Pegu 576
Peking see Beijing
Pelayo 184
Peloponnesian wars 82, 83, 85, 90
Peloponnesus 40, 49, 55
Pembroke, Richard de Clare, Earl of ("Strongbow") 250, **251**, *251*
Penang 515, 519
Pencils, invention of 379

Thirty Years' War 414–415, 417, 419, 424, 433
  war with Denmark 433
  war with Poland 438
  Treaty of Kardis 443
  Great Northern War 456–457, **466–467**, 471, 473
  Seven Years' War 496
Sweyn I Forkbead, King of Denmark 211, 214, 217, 218, 222
Sweyn I, King of Norway 222
Sweyn II, King of Denmark 222
Swift, Jonathan 494
Swiss Confederation 331, 332, 353
Switzerland:
  Reformation 355
  civil war 361
  Calvinism 366
  Villmergen wars 438
  World War II 693
Swords 235, 314, *314*
Syagrius 152
Sydney *541*
Sydney Harbour Bridge *654*
Sylvester, Pope 200, *201*
Syria:
  Hittite invasion 40
  Seleucid dynasty 79, 94
  Romans conquer 103, 112
  Arabs conquer 176, 177
  in Ottoman empire 355
  war with Ottoman Turks 565
  independence from France 639, 704
  French mandate 658
  Druse uprising 670
  World War II 694
Szalankemen, battle of (1691) 465

T

Tabei, Junko 734
Tabriz, battle of (1604) 399, 402
Tacitus, Emperor 135
Tahiti 79, 152, 239, 257, 559, 569, 615
T'ai Tsung the Great, Emperor of China 177, 211
Taikwa reforms, Japan 178
Taiping rebellion 559, *568*, 569, 572
Taira clan 254–255
Taiwan 616, 716, 734
  see also Formosa
Taj Mahal *401*, 413, 423, 440, *441*
The Tale of Genji 199
Talleyrand, Charles Maurice de 542
Talmud 178
Tamerlane *241*, *272–273*, 272–273, 291, 295, 299, 302, 304, 360
Tammany Hall 541
Tamyris 74
T'ang, Emperor of China 43
Tang dynasty 159, *159*, *161*, **170–171**, 174, *181*, *197*, 203, 232
Tanganyika 658
  see also Tanzania
Tanganyika, Lake 593, 635
Tangier 182, 329, 443

Tanis 50
Tanks 657, 712, *712*
Tannenberg, battle of (1914) 642
Tanzania 658, 714, 718, 726
Taoism 104
Tapestries 246, **436**, *436*
Tarquinius Superbus, King of Rome 74
Tartars 290, 318, 336, 382, 383
Taruga 133
Tarxien 31
Tasman, Abel 399, 430, **454**, *454*
Tasmania 76, 399, 454, *540*, 559, 579, 630–631
Tassili-n-Ajjer *59*
Taxation:
  Poll Tax 299
  window-tax *493*
Taxila *90*, 149
Tchaikovsky, Peter Ilyich 599
Tea 427, **429**, *429*, 433, 450, 503, 515, *549*
Tea ceremony 393
Tear gas 633
Technology *see* Science and technology
Tecumseh 538, *538*, 539
Tehuacan Valley 31
Telamon, battle of (225 B.C.) 98
Telegraph 501, *501*, 529, 588
Telephones 588, 589, *589*, 596, 611, 645
Telescopes 408, *446*, *452*, 453
Television 660, *661*, 670, 740
Telstar 740
Temple of Heaven, Beijing *481*, *493*
Temple Mound culture 158, 182, *182*
Temples:
  Egyptian *21*
  ancient Greece *93*
  Mayan *93*
Temujin *see* Genghis Khan
Temur Oljaitu, Emperor of China *273*
Teng, Dowager Empress 126
Tennis 357, 596
Tennyson, Alfred 572
Tenochtitlán 238, 240, *278*, 279, 283, 320, 322–323, *322*, 340, 358, 362–363, *362*, *380*
Tensing Norgay 722
Teotihuacán 77, 78, 93, *134*, *134*, 135, 158, 208
Tereshkova, Valentina 725
Terracotta army *99*
Terrorism 730, 733, 737
Tertry, battle of (687) 182
Test Acts 443, 450, 458
Test-tube baby 737
Teusina, Treaty of (1595) 393
Teutonic Knights 326
Teutonic tribes 57
Tewkesbury, battle of (1471) 329
Texas 368, 491, 557, 558, **562–563**, 569
Texcoco, Lake 279
Thai peoples 120
Thailand 726
  prehistory 11, 79

ancient history 27
invades Cambodia *241*, 310, 311
World War II 696
military coup 737
see also Siam
Thames river 12, 214, 418, 449, *449*
Thanksgiving Day *397*, **409**
Thatcher, Margaret 738, 744
Theater:
  Greek and Roman *116*, 117
  Middle Ages 246
  Elizabethan England 325
  commedia dell'arte 435
  actresses 443
  pantomime 471
  18th century 484
  19th century 566
Thebes (Egypt) 42, 54, 70
Thebes (Greece) 89
Theodora, Empress 162, **163**, *164*
Theodoric the Great, King of the Ostrogoths 151, 152, 156
Theodosius, General 143
Theodosius I the Great, Emperor 143
Theodosius II, Emperor 144
Thera 10, 38, 39, 42
Thermometers 453, *453*, 487
Thermopylae, battle of (480 B.C.) 82, 83
Thevenot, Jean 446
Thirty-Nine Articles 379
Thirty Tyrants 135
Thirty Years' War 371, 397, 398, 414–415, **416–417**, 418, 419, 423, 424, 430, 433, 435, 437, 473
Thompson, John 659
Thomson, Joseph John 620
Thor 204, 217
Thorn, Peace of (1466) 326
Thorpe, Jim 635
The Thousand and One Nights 191, *191*, 201
Thrace 90
Thucydides 1, 88
Thuringia 182
Thutmosis I, Pharaoh 40
Thutmosis II, Pharaoh 42
Thutmosis III, Pharaoh 42, 54
Tiahuanaco 158, 208–209, 229
Tianjin 687, 716
Tiber River 66
Tiberius, Emperor 119, 121
Tibet:
  Mongol invasions 270, 188
  Dalai Lama **433**, 445
  China takes control of 491
Tientsin Treaty (1858) **581**
Tientsin Treaty (1885) *605*
Tiffany, Louis *566*
Tiglathpileser I, King of Assyria 48, 55
Tiglathpileser III, King of Assyria 48, 64
Tigris River 9, 18, 24, 25, 48, 126, 135
Tikal *80*, 93
Tilly, Count 423, 424
Timbuktu 264, *264*, 310, 326, 340, 344–345, *345*, 598
Time bombs 391
The Times 520

Timur *360*
Tinchebrai, battle of (1106) 242
Tintoretto *324*
Tipu Sultan 479, 519, *528*, *529*, 532
Titanic 635
Titian 324
Titicaca, Lake 208
Titicaca basin 327
Tito, Marshal 703, **705**, *705*, 738
Titus, Emperor 122, 126
Tiwanaku culture 78
Tlaloc *16*, 134
Tobacco 376, 379, 408, **409**, 414, *469*, 476, 549, *549*
Tobago 446
Tobruk 694
Toghril Beg 230
Tokugawa shoguns 514, 578, 586
Tokyo 586
  see also Edo
Tolbiac, battle of (496) 152
Toledo 144, 232
Toleration Act (1689) 463
"Tollund Man" 3
Tolstoy, Leo 567, 590
Toltecs 158, 160, *160*, 165, 208, *208*, 209, 238, 248
Tombaugh, Clyde 675
Tombs:
  prehistoric 20
  Egyptian 5
  mastabas 27, *27*
  megaliths *31*
  barrows 31
  "beehive" 40–41, *40*
Tomsk 402
Tonga 11, 152, 399, 454, 714
Tonkin 121, 482, 604, *605*
Tonle Sap 310
Tools:
  prehistoric 14
  for building 20
  in the ancient world 52
  in the classical world 92, *92*
  farming 188
  see also Science and technology
Topa, Sapa Inca 318, 322, 326, 327, 329
Topiltzin Quetzalcoatl 208
Toqtamish 299
Tordesillas, Treaty of (1494) 318, 344
Tories 455
Toronto 539
Torpedoes 555
Torres, Luis Vaez de 399
Torres Strait 399
Torricelli, Evangelista 433, 453
Tostig, Earl of Northumbria 225, 227
Totem poles *164*
Toul 371, 376
Toulouse 263
Toulouse-Lautrec, Henri de 609
Touraine 248, 258
Tournaments 244, 245
Toussaint L'Ouverture, Pierre Dominique *480*, 526–527, *526–527*, 544
Toutswe state 158
Tower of London 173, 227, 326, 329, 339

Ur 11, 24, 25, *25*, 33, 39
Uranus (planet) 725
Urban II, Pope 232, 242
Urban IV, Pope 267
Urban VI, Pope 296–297
Urban VIII, Pope 417
Urbino, Duke of 336, 337
Ursuline nuns 357
Uruguay 584, 590
Uruk 24, 31, 33
USSR:
  creation of 664
  civil war 652, 659, 663
  farming 668, 669, *698*
  Five-Year Plans 672
  Great Purge 681
  World War II 638, 692–695
  end of World War II 700–701
  blockades Berlin 710
  COMECON 714
  suppresses Hungarian Rising 718, 722, 725
  Cuban missile crisis 718, 723, 726
  invades Czechoslovakia 718, 722, *722*, 730
  nuclear weapons 718, 742
  space travel 718, 720, *721*, **724–725**, 726, 733
  invades Afghanistan 719, 722, 738
  Cold War 720, **722–723**, 724
  nuclear power 722
  shoots down U-2 spy plane 726
  civil rights movement 737
  withdraws from Afghanistan 742
  attempted coup 744
  collapse of 718, **738–739**, 744
  rulers 755
  see also Russia
Utah 563, 571
Uthman dan Fodio 507, *507*, 536
Utica 10, 50, 62
Utopia (More) *381*
Utrecht, Peace of (1713) 439, *470*, 471, 478, 482
Utrecht, Union of 386
Uzan Hasan 331
Uzbekistan 230

V

V-1 flying bombs 701
V-2 rocket bombs 701
Vaccination 488, 531, *535*, 576, *607*, *675*, *685*, 740
Vadimo, Lake, battle of (310 B.C.) 94
Valencia 683
Valens, Emperor 143, 144
Valentinian I, Emperor 143
Valentinian III, Emperor 146
Valentino, Rudolph 670
Valerian, Emperor *130*, 131, 135
Valetta *384*
Valley of the Kings 55
Valois dynasty *215*, 286
Valtelline Pass 417
Van Diemen, Anthony 454
Van Diemen's Land 430, 454, 559, 579, 630–631

Van Dyck, Sir Anthony 404, 424
Van Gogh, Vincent 611
Vanbrugh, John 413
Vancouver, George 523
Vancouver Island 593
Vandals 78, *142*, 143, 144, 145, 146, 151, 152, 155, 167, 182
Vanuatu 714
Varaharan V, King of Persia 146
Vasili III, Grand Prince of Muscovy 382
Vatican City 666
  Sistine Chapel 325, 331, 350
Vauban, Sébastien de *472*
Vaults 127, *127*
Vauxhall Gardens, London *551*
Vedas 65
Veii 89
Velázquez, Diego de Silva y 404, *423*
Venezuela 537, 539, 551, 626
Venice 258–259, 355, 586, 591
  foundation of 151
  trade 211, 237, 256
  Great Council 248
  government 300
  banks *309*
  wars with Ottoman Turks 319, 322, 331, 383, 384, 385, 399, 433, 438, 449
  alliance with Florence and Milan 331
  pays tribute to Ottoman empire 336
  in the Renaissance 336
  Aldine Press 340, *343*
  Holy League 344, 353, 458
  doges 259, *381*
  attacks Athens 458
Venus (planet) 724, 733
Venus de Milo 95, *95*
Venus of Willendorf **15**
Vercingetorix 112–113, *113*, 115
Verdi, Giuseppe 572, 576, 593
Verdun 371, 376
Verdun, battle of (1916) 644, 648
Verdun, Treaty of (843) 195
Vereeniging Treaty (1902) 626
Vermeer, Jan *429*
Verne, Jules 590
Verrocchio 331
Versailles 397, *401*, 412, 413, *436* 437, *437*, *438*, 443, *496*, 523
Versailles Peace Settlement and Treaty (1919) 638, 656, 658–659, *658*, 680, 681, *682*, 688–689
Vesalius, Andreas 368, 372
Vespasian, Emperor 119, 122
Vespucci, Amerigo 340, *341*, 346, 350
Vesuvius, Mount 126
Vichy France 694, *695*
Victor Emmanuel II, King of Italy 583, **590**, *590*
Victor Emmanuel III, King of Italy 664, 704
Victoria, Lake 581

Victoria, Queen of England 562, *566*, 572, 576, *580*, **580–581**, 599, 610, 623
Victoria and Albert Museum, London 576
Vienna:
  Ottoman Turks besiege 318, 359, 361, 399, 455, *455*, 456, 473
  Hungary captures 339
  Schonbrunn palace *482*
  1848 uprising 571
  German troops in *689*
Vienna, Congress of (1815) **542**
Vienna, Treaty of (1725) 494
Vienna, Treaty of (1731) 497
Vietnam:
  Chinese conquest 79
  conquers the Champa 319
  Annamese 329
  Cambodians evacuate Saigon 466
  French colony 604
  independence from France 714
  Vietnam War 719, 723, 726, 727, 729, 730, 733, 734
  invades Cambodia 719, 737
  Communists control 734
  unification 737
Vijaya 239
Vikings 187, **216–219**
  sagas 6
  religion 157, 204, *205*
  villages *157*
  in Normandy 158
  in North America *160*, 254
  arts and crafts 165, *192*, *196*
  longships *165*, *228*
  in Russia 184–185, 198, 229
  as farmers 188, 189
  invasions of England 190, 192, 195, 198, 202–203, 217, *217*, 234
  in Scotland 194, *194*
  in Ireland 195, 217, 218, 229, 250
  in Constantinople 197
  settle in Iceland 198, 205
  in Greenland 201
  cremations *204*
  Eric the Red 211
  government 220
  coins *228*
  trade 228
  warfare *234–235*
Villages 172
Villanova culture 57
Villas, Roman *105*
Villeins 225
Villmergen wars 438
Vincennes 498
Vinegar Hill 532
Vinland 6, 218
Violins 371, 446
Virgil 112
Virgin Islands 427
Virginia 318, *349*, 391, 393, 398, 407, 408, 411, 418, 429, *460*, 469, 476, 545, *545*
Virginia City *617*
Virginia Company *411*
Vishnu 97, *136*
Visigoths 143, 144, 145, 155, 156, 162, 171, 182, 184

Vitellius, Emperor 122
Vitoria, battle of (1813) 542
Vittorio Veneto, battle of (1918) 652
Vivaldi, Antonio 494
Vladimir, Grand Prince of Kiev *184*, 185, 214
Vladislav, Prince of Poland 408
Vladislav of Poland, King of Bohemia 329
Volagases of Persia 151
Volga River 203, 264
Volkswagen cars *661*
Volta, Alessandro 532, *535*
Voltaire, François Marie Arouet de *504*, 505, *511*
Volunteers, World War I *643*
Votes for women 590, 615, **626–627**, 659, 672, *698*, *699*
Voyager (airplane) *741*

W

Wagner, Richard 566, 567, 599
Wagons 34
Wahhabism 524, 525
Wailing Wall, Jerusalem *110*
Waitangi, Treaty of (1840) 559, 565, 572, *572*
Wakefield, battle of (1460) 312
Waldseemuller, Martin 350
Wales:
  coracles 52
  Christianity in 168
  Aethelflaed fights in 207
  English forced out of 267
  English conquest 273
  Owen Glendower's rebellion 302, 304
  Act of Union (1801) 536
  see also Britain
Walesa, Lech 738
Wall paintings 4, *137*
Wall Street Crash (1929) 637, 638, 672, *678*, 679, *699*, 706
Wallace, William 274–275, 279, 281
Wallachia 571, 576, 577, 583
Wallenstein, Count 417, 418, 423
Walpole, Sir Robert 491
Walter the Penniless 242
Walworth, William 299
Wampanoag Indians 409, *450*
Wampum (shell beads) 469
Wan Li, Emperor of China 384
Wang Anshi 227, 232
Wang Mang 121
Wanggon 207
War and weapons:
  China 43
  in the ancient world **68–69**
  catapults **90**, *90*
  Roman army **114–115**
  499 B.C.–A.D. 500 **154–155**
  "Greek fire" *163*
  501–1100 A.D. **234–235**
  Crusades **242–243**
  knights 242, **244–245**
  samurai 255, *255*
  Mongols *271*, *272*
  crossbows **287**, *287*

Acknowledgments

The publishers would like to thank the following artists for their contribution to this book:

Jonathan Adams 441*b*; Hemesh Alles (Maggie Mundy) 260*b*, 356*b*, 393*m*, 405*tr*, 421*br*, 425*m*, 434*br*, 435*br*, 453*r*, 459*tl*, 460*t*, 461*r*, 464*b*, 468*t*, 495*t*, 503*mr*, 514*b*, 521*t*, 523*t*, 525*ml*, 546, 571*l*, 583, 591, 592–593, 598*b*, 602*mr*, 605, 616*b*, 618*t*, 623*t*, 631*t*, 633*mr*, 665*b*, 704*b*, 716*b*; Marion Appleton 63*tr*, 101*ml*, 148*t*, 164*m*, 166*t*, 170*t*, 181*b*, 233*br*, 259*br*, 323*tl*, 324, 356*t*, 394*m*, 404*m*, 439*b*, 444*t*, 446*b*, 453*l*, 457*tr*, 460*bl*, 484*m,b*, 485*t*, 505*b*, 514*ml*, 516*t*, 519*t*, 530*m,l*, 531*t*, 544*b*, 566*tl*, 566*m,b*, 567*l*, 573*m*, 589*b*, 603*tl*, 606*m*, 612*mr*, 619*m*, 624*m*, 632*t,m*, 633*tl*, 646*t,b*, 647*m*, 676*t*, 681, 690*t*, 715*tr*; Sue Barclay 123*b*; R. Barnett 431*b*; Noel Bateman 205*r*; Simon Bishop 662*b*; Richard Bonson 96*bl*, 153*m*, 269*m*, 279*b*, 310*t*, 323*b*, 428*t,b*, 468*m*, 508*m*, 393*t*; Nick Cannan 28*b,t*; Vanessa Card 12, 17*t*, 28*t*, 29*b*, 45*tl*, 47*b*, 51*tr*, 59*tr*, 59*b*, 87*mr*, 89*bl*, 116*tl*, 129*t*, 137*t*, 138*t*, 163*b*, 164*br*, 167*m*, 167*b*, 173*t*, 179*t*, 180*t*, 183*bl*, 187*ml*, 188*b*, 191*tl, br*, 198*b*, 200*b*, 204*ml*, 221*t*, 226*t*, 229*t*, 245*t*, 249*b*, 254*b*, 266*t*, 276*br*, 279, 292*t,b*, 300*b*, 308*b*, 309*b*, 311*t*, 349*m*, 351*t*, 357*t*, 358*b*, 361*b*, 364*m*, 372*tr*, 376*t*, 392*t*, 396, 402*b*, 422*t*, 424*m*, 425*b*, 435*tl*, 436*m*, 441*t*, 445*br*, 455*b*, 457*t*, 469*t*, 503*b*, 505*tr*, 515*m*, 524*b*, 526*b*, 529, 541*t,ml*, 555, 568*m,b*, 609, 610, 618*m*, 623*b*, 653*tr*, 668*t*, 698*m*; Tony Chance (Garden Studio) 601*b*, 631*br*; Harry Clow 565*b*, 673*b*; Stephen Conlin 20*b*, 25*t*, 33*m*, 45*mr*, 60*mr*, 166*b*, 270*m*, 460*b*, 476*b*, 507*b*, 575*m*; Peter Dennis (Linda Rogers Assoc.) 500*m*, 501*mr*, 509*t*, 543, 549*t*, 553*b*; Dave Etchell 252*m*, 530*br*; James Field (Simon Girling Assoc.) 108*bl*, 109*mr*, 250*b*, 275*b*, 289*b*, 294*b*, 487*ml*, 496–497*t*, 534–535*b*; Michael Fisher 311*b*, 413*b*; Eugene Fleury All maps; Chris Forsey 37*t,br*, 60*tr*, 61*m*, 86*mr*, 87*tl*, 125*b*, 134*t,bl*, 145*t*, 196*mr*, 234*m*, 235*mr*, 262*t*, 282*b*, 469*m*, 492*m*, 508*b*, 548, 555, 692*t*; Dewey Franklin (Garden Studio) 562*b*, 567*t*; Terry Gabbey (Eva Morris A.F.A) 16*m*, 17*m*, 22*b*, 23*ml*, 42*br*, 43*bl*, 44*tr,tl,bl*, 45*ml*, 51*b*, 62*b*, 84*t*, 87*ml*, 91*t*, 101*ml*, 111*br*, 113*m*, 124*b*, 130*t*, 140*b* 154*b*, 164*bl*, 165*tl*, 187*t*, 193*b*, 199*r*, 201*t*, 204*br*, 207*t*, 208*t*, 212*bl*, 231*t*, 234, 235*b,tr*, 236*b*, 247*ml*, 253*br*, 256*b*, 259*ml*, 280*t*, 293*m*, 295*m*, 303*tr*, 313*b*, 326*bl*, 331*t*, 349*b*, 369*b*, 388*m*, 405*m*, 432*t*, 447*t*, 451*r*, 473*mr*, 482*b*, 554, 527*t*, 538*b*, 570*b*, 600*b*, 617*b*; Fred Gambino 573*t*; John Gillatt 490*t*; Jeremy Gower 132*br*; Neil Gower 172*m*; Ray Grinaway 285*ml*, 517*m*, 585*b*, 621*t*, 632*bl*, 635, 653*b*, 658*m*, 711*tr*, 713*bl*; Allan Hardcastle 120*t*, 275*mr*, 295*b*, 305*tl*, 371*b*; Nick Harris 11; Nicholas Hewetson 2, 5*m*, 36*m*, 37*ml*, 43*tr*, 52*t*, 53*br*, 61*t*, 86*ml*, 99*m*, 100*bl*, 106*bl*, 130*b*, 132*ml*, 145*b*, 150*b*, 154*t*, 169*b*, 195*b*, 206*b*, 211*t*, 213*tr,b*, 220*b*, 224, 235*tl*, 244*t*, 247*t*, 255*t*, 276*bl*, 277*b*, 284*t*, 293*b,tr*, 301*tr*, 315*tr*, 323*tl*, 342*tl* 353*b*, 355*t*, 357*ml*, 369*tr*, 370*t*, 393*b*, 404*b*, 416*t*, 434*t*, 450*m*, 460*m*, 462*b* ,472*m*, 473*tl*, 515*b*,

525*mr*, 664*b*, 711*tl*, 725; Bruce Hogarth 620–621*b*; Richard Hook 95*b*, 116*b*, 119*t*,120*b*, 123*t*, 243*bl*, 244*b*, 316*b*, 377*b*, 436*b*, 577; Simon Huson 15*t*, 16*b*, 63*b*, 124*ml*, 741*bl*; John James (Pat Kelliner) 183*t*, 219*b*, 364*t*, 380*t*, 390*t*, 391*m*, 397, 409*t*, 410*b*, 475*b*, 518*b*, 557; Peter Jarvis (Simon Girling Assoc.) 384*b*, 587*b*, 624*b*; Deborah Kindred (Simon Girling Assoc.) 92*t*, 93*b*, 119*b*, 128*t*, 135*b*, 173*ml*, 175*b*, 189*mr*, 253*tr*, 261*t*, 280*bl*, 284*m*, 285*t*, 290*b*, 297*t*, 330*t*, 347*b*, 383*t*, 597*b*, 614*t*; Adrian Lascome 366*b*; Jason Lewis 152*b*, 263*t*, 266*b*, 273*b*, 287*tl*, 292*m*, 301*tll*, 325*t*, 334*tll*, 341*b*, 348*t*, 372*tl*, 381*t*, 410*m*, 413*t*, 420–421*m*; Chris Lyon 713*br*; Kevin Maddison 5*b*, 14*m*, 18*b*, 19*b*, 22*m*, 22*b*, 27*b*, 36*t*, 37*mr*, 52*m*, 53*t*, 54*bl*, 56*t*, 57*bl*, 59*tl*, 63*tl*, 73*b*, 75*m*, 86*b*, 89*bl*, 92*bl*, 102*b*, 103*b*, 105*tr*, 116*tr*, 117*tr*, *tl*, 121*t*, 131*b*, 132*b*, 142*m*, 151*b*, 163*ml*, 189*b*, 202*t*, 208*br*, 218, 219, 245*b*, 247*ml*, 294*t*, 302*b*, 345*t*, 348*bl*, 362*b*, 527, 536*b*, 544*mr*, 578*t*, 583; Shirley Mallinson 506*b*; Shane Marsh 407*b*; David MacAllister 328*b*, 389*b*, 419*t*; Angus McBride (Linden Artists) 9*b*, 14*t*, 15*b*, 21*b*, 25*b*, 31*b*, 35*t*, 44–45*b*, 48*b*, 61*b*, 68*b*, 69*b*, 113*b*, 128*b*, 303*b*; Frank Nichols 389*t*; Chris D. Orr 364*b*, 365*b*, 373*b*, 394*t*, 403*m*, 407*m*, 412*t*, b, 433*t*, 444*m*, 475*t*, 493*tl*, b, 550, 575*t*, 654*m*, 715*b*; Sharon Pallent 41*tr*; R. Payne 305*tr*; R. Philips 317*b*; Jayne Pickering 409*m*, Melvyn Pickering 39*b*, 46*mr*, 66*t*, 68*tl*, 132*t*, 138*ml*, 148*mr*; Malcolm Porter 13, 29; Mike Posen 608; John Ridyard 490*b*, 509*br*; Mike Roffe 489*m*, 496*mr*, 500*t*, 501*br*, 549, 528*t*, 534*m*, 712*m*; Chris Rothero 63*ml*; David Salarya 24, 26, 41, 54, 72, 84, 83, 88, 103, 108, 109, 117, 128, 159, 148, 157, 165, 169, 194, 196, 197, 202, 204, 221, 226, 229; Mike Saunders 607*tr*; Rodney Shackell All biography box heads, 32*b*, 53*m*, 63*ml*, 64*b*, 101*b*, 104*b*, 106*t*, 107*t*, 115*bl*, 125*r*, 132*ml*, 133*ml*, 172*t*, 173*b*, 210, 243*br*, 257, 277*t*, 288*b*, 293*tl*, 296*b*, 308*m*, 325*bl*, 367*t*, 372*b*, 378*t*, 406*b*, 439*r*, 441*mr*, 456*b*; Rob Shone 5*t*, 21*t*, 52*tr*, 52*br*, 54*t*, 65*t*, 95*tl*, 96*bl*, 101*t*, 102*t*, 109*t*, 124*mr*, 133*mr*, 137*m*, 139*t*, 147*ml*, 149*t*, 151*t*, 155*m*, 156*b*, 174*b*, 179*br*, 181*tl*, 188*m*, 189*ml*, 190*b*, 191*mr*, 196*bl*, 208*b*, 212*t*, 220*t*, 230*b*, 233*bl*, 249*tr*, 258*b*, 261*b*, 269*t*, 291*b*, 309*mr*, 343*tr*, 365*ml*, 387*b*, 417*b*, 435*tr*, 446*m*, 447*l*, 452*t*, 474*b*, 576, 579*t*, 588*bl*, 593, 594*m*, 595*b*, 597*bl*, 602*t*, 607*b*, 612*ml*, 613, 618–619*b*, 626*b*, 633*b*, 636, 684*m*, 724*b, t*, 735*t*; Mark Stacey 511, 540*b*; Paul Stangroom 499*b*, 516*b*, 524*t*, 541*br*; Stephen Sweet 669*t*, *b*; Mike Taylor (Simon Girling Assoc.) 261*m*, 306*t*, 415*t*, 428*bl*, 434*bl*; George Thompson 122*b*, 356*m*, 429*r*; David Wright (Kathy Jakeman) 189*ml*, 237*r*; Paul Wright 365*mr*, 555, 564*t*, 630*m*.

Additional black and white illustrations by: Chris Lenthall, Stefan Morris, Jackie Moore, Branka Surla, Smiljka Surla, John Kelly, Martin Wilson, Teresa Morris, Matthew Gore, Ian Fish.

The publishers wish to thank the following for supplying photographs for this book:

Page 1 *t* ZEFA, *b* Press Association; 2 ZEFA; 3 National Museum, Denmark; 4 *t* Michael Holford, *b* Cambridge University Collection of Air Photographs; 6 British Museum; 7 *t* Peter Newark Photographs, *b* ZEFA; 8 *l* E.T. Archive, *r* Mansell Collec tion; 12 ZEFA; 16 Reunion des Musees Nationaux; 17 *l* Brooklyn Museum, *r* Reunion des Musees Nationaux; 25 ZEFA; 26 Peter Clayton; 28 Peter Clayton; 30 ZEFA; 60 British Museum; 69 Ancient Art and Architecture Collection; 76 ZEFA; 81 Michael Holford; 88 Ancient Art and Architecture Collection; 110 and 111 Sonia Halliday Photographs; 125 Sonia Halliday Photographs; 133 Mansell Collection; 142 Sonia Halliday Photographs; 149 C.M. Dixon; 156 Trinity College, Cambridge; 164 Sonia Halliday Photographs; 169 Trinity College, Dublin; 177 Sonia Halliday Photographs; 179 Ancient Art and Architechture Collection; 180 Mansell Collection; 181 British Library; 183 ZEFA; 185 Michael Holford; 192 British Museum; 196 Michael Holford; 197 Werner Forman Archive; 205 ZEFA; 212 Bodleian Library; 215 Mansell Collection; 222 and 223 Town of Bayeux; 227 Public Record Office; 228 Seattle Art Museum; 229 Werner Forman Archive; 233 E.T. Archive; 235 Werner Forman Archive; 241 Giraudon; 243 Sonia Halliday Photographs; 246 Sonia Halliday Photo graphs; 247 National Gallery, London; 251 National Gallery of Ireland; 259 Bodleian Library; 262 Mary Evans Picture Library; 264 British Library; 274 Scottish National Portrait Gallery; 277 National Gallery, London; 284 Michael Holford; 287 Bodleian Library; 291 SCALA; 298 British Library; 299 Giraudon; 300 Windsor Castle, Royal Library 1992 Her Majesty The Queen; 303 ZEFA; 308 Giraudon; 309 British Library; 314 Werner Forman Archive; 321 Michael Holford; 323 SCALA; 324 *t* National Gallery, *b* V & A/Bridgeman Art Library; 327 South American Pictures; 329 Michael Holford; 332 SCALA; 333 *t* Galleria degli Uffizi/Bridgeman Art Library, *m* Mary Evans Picture Library; 334 Michael Holford; 337 SCALA; 343 *l* St. Bride Library, *r* SCALA; 345 Mary Evans Picture Library; 347 E.T. Archive; 348 Michael Holford; 349 Christie's/Bridgeman Art Library; 351 National Portrait Gallery; 352 Michael Holford; 353 Werner Forman Archive; 357 V & A/Bridgeman Art Library; 360 Michael Holford; 365 British Museum; 368 Mary Evans Picture Library; 372 Mary Evans Picture Library; 373 Ann Ronan Picture Library; 375 By kind permission of the Marquess of Tavistock and the Trustees of the Bedford Estates; 378 Giraudon; 381 *m* National Gallery, *b* Mansell Collection; 382 fotomas Index; 385 National Maritime Museum; 387 E.T. Archive; 388 *t* Giraudon/Bridgeman Art Library, *b* Bibliotheque Nationale/Bridgeman Art Library; 389 British Library; 391 Mary Evans Picture Library; 395 *t* Werner Forman Archive, *b* The Royal Collection/St. James' Palace c H M Queen; 401 Mary Evans Picture Library; 403 Mary Evans Picture Library; 404 *t*, Rijkmuseum, *b* Bridgeman Art Library; 405 *b* British Museum; 406 National Portrait Gallery; 410 Mansell Collection; 412 Spectrum; 420 Michael Holford; 421 Hulton-Deutsch Collection; 422 *l* Mansell Collection, *r* Michael Holford; 423 Prado/ Bridgeman Art Library; 47 Rijkmuseum; 428 Mansell Collection; 429 Staatliche Kunstsammlungen/Bridgeman Art Library; 431 British Museum; 432 Fotomas Index; 435 V&A/Bridgeman Art Library; 437 Mary Evans Picture Library; 440 Mary Evans Picture Library; 444 Fotomas Index; 445 *t* Sonia Halliday Photo graphs, *b* Peter Newark Photographs; 447 The Hague; 448 National Maritime Museum; 451 National Maritime Museum; 452 *bl* Michael Holford, *br* Ann Ronan Picture Library; 453 Mansell Collection; 454 Mansell Collection; 457 Spectrum; 458 Peter Clayton; 459 Mansell Collection; 461 *t* E.T. Archive, *b* Giraudon/ Bridgeman Art Library; 463 Peter Newark Photographs; 465 National Portrait Gallery; 467 Kungil Armemuseum; 469 *l* Bank of England, *b* Mansell Collection; 472 National Army Museum; 473 Fotomas Index; 477 Mansell Collection; 483 V&A/Bridgeman Art Library; 484 *t* Michael Holford, *b* SCALA; 485 *r* British Library/Bridgeman Art Library, *l* V&A/Bridgeman Art Library; 486 E.T. Archive; 489 *t* Ann Ronan Picture Library, *b* Holkham Estate; 491 Mansell Collection; 493 Mary Evans Picture Library; 494 Ancient Art & Architecture Collection; 495 India Office Library/Bridgeman Art Library; 499 National Army Museum; 501 Mansell Collection; 504 Tate Gallery/Bridgeman Art Library; 505 Giraudon; 507 Mary Evans Picture Library; 508 E.T. Archive; 509 Ann Ronan Picture Library; 510 Michael Holford; 512 Michael Holford; 514 *t* V&A/Bridgeman Art Library, *b* Mansell Collection; 515 National Gallery; 517 Michael Holford; 521 Peter Newark Pictures; 523 Giraudon; 524 Mansell Collection; 525 E.T. Archive; 528 Guildhall Library/Bridgeman Art Library; 534 Mansell Collection; 535 *ml*

E.T. Archive, *mr* Lindley Library, R H S/Bridgeman Art Library, *br* Science Museum; 539 Bettiman Archive; 50 *t* Prado/Bridgeman Art Library, *m* E.T. Archive; 541 Mansell Collection; 544 Peter Newark Pictures; 545 Peter Newark Pictures; 546 Mansell Collection; 547 Mansell Collection; 548 Mansell Collection; 549 *l* Werner Forman Archive, *b* City of Bristol Museum & Art Gallery/Bridgeman Art Library; 551 Guildhall Library/Bridgeman Art Library; 552 Windsor Castle, Royal Library 1992 Her Majesty The Queen; 554 Peter Newark Pictures; 556 Peter Newark Pictures; 561 Mary Evans Picture Library; 563 Betmann Archive; 564 Mary Evans Picture Library; 566 *t* Allans of Duke Street, London, DACS/Hermitage, St. Petersburg,*r* Bridgeman Art Library; 569 National Army Musem; 572 New Zealand High Commission/Bridgeman Art Library; 573 Royal Geographical Society/Bridgeman Art Library; 574 Mary Evans Picture Library; 575 Mary Evans Picture; 578 Kyoto Costume Institute; 580 Windsor Castle, Royal Library Her Majesty The Queen; 585 Peter Newark Pictures; 588 *r* Mansell Collection, *b* Mary Evans Picture Library; 589 *ml*, *br* Mary Evans Picture Library; 594 *t* Science Museum, *b* Mansell Collection; 599 Mary Evans Picture Library; 600 Mary Evans Picture Library; 602 *bl* Science Museum; 603 Christopher Wood Gallery/Bridgeman Art Library; 604 Giraudon; 606 Mary Evans Picture Library; 607 Mansell Collection; 609 Mary Evans Picture Library; 611 Mary Evans Picture Library; 612 Mansell Collection; 613 Peter Newark Pictures; 614 Library of Congress; 617 Peter Newark Pictures; 619 Trades Union Congress; 622 Bettmann Archive; 624 Mary Evans Pic ture Library; 625 Mary Evans Picture Library; 627 *t* E.T. Archive, *b* E.T. Archive; 629 *t* Novosti Press Agency, *b* Victoria & Albert Museum; 636 Mansell Collection; 637 Peter Newark Pictures; 640 *t* Imperial War Museum, *b* ZEFA; 641 *t* E.T. Archive, *bl* Sonia Halliday Photographs; 642 E.T. Archive; 643 *t* E.T. Archive, *b* Mary Evans Picture Library; 644 *t* Imperial War Museum, *b* E.T. Archive; 645 E.T. Archive; 646 *r* E.T. Archive, *br* Ronald Grant Archive; 647 *tr* Visual Arts Library, *b* Galerie Der Stadt Stuttgart; 648 Hulton-Deutsch Collection; 649 *t* Mary Evans Pic ture Library, *b* Hulton-Deutsch Collection; 650 Novosti Press Agency; 652 Bettmann Archive; 654 *t* Architectural Association/Taylor Galyean, *b* E.T. Archive; 655 *l* Architectural Association/Andrew Higgot, *r* ZEFA; 656 Imperial War Museum; 657 Imperial War Museum; 658 *t* Illustrated London News, *b* Bettmann Archive; 660 *t* Mary Evans Picture Library, *m* Illustrated London News, *b* Peter Newark Pictures; *tl* 661 B.B.C., *tr* Hulton-Deutsch Collection, *ml/bl* ZEFA, *mr* E.T. Archive; 662 Peter Newark Pictures; 665 Sonia Halliday Photographs; 666 *t* E.T. Archive, *b* Popperfoto; 667 Peter Newark Photographs; 668 Bettmann Archive; 669 Bettmann Archive; 671 Bettmann Archive; 674 Bettmann Archive; 675 Popperfoto; 676 *m* E.T. Archive, *b* Peter Newark Pictures; 677 *tl* Ronald Grant Archive, *tr* Mary Evans Picture Library, *m* Peter Newark Pictures, *b* Imperial War Museum; 678 Bettmann Archive; 679 Popperfoto; 680 *t* Imperial War Museum, *b* Peter Newark Pictures; 681 Bettmann Archive; 682 E.T. Archive; 683 *m* Bettmann Archive, *b* Popperfoto; 684 *t* ZEFA, *b* Science Photo Library; 685 *t* Popperfoto, *b* Bettmann Archive; 686 Bettmann Ar chive; 687 Bettmann Archive; 688 Popperfoto; 689 *t* E.T. Archive, *m* Peter Newark Pictures, *b* Hulton-Deutsch Collection; 690 E.T. Archive; 691 *t* IBM/ENIAC, *m* Popperfoto, *bl* Liberty Archive, Victoria Library/Bridgeman Art Library, *br* Ronald Grant Archive; 693 Imperial War Museum; 694 Imperial War Museum; 695 Peter Newark Pictures; 696 Bettmann Archive; 697 *l* E.T. Archive, *r* Bettmann Archive; 698 *t* Popperfoto, *b* Hulton-Deutsch Collection; 699 *t,m* Bettmann Archive, *b* Hul ton-Deutsch Collection; 700 Bettmann Archive; 701 Imperial War Museum; 702 *l* United Nations, *r* Bettmann Archive; 703 *t* United Nations, *b* ZEFA; 706 *t,m* Mary Evans Picture Library, *b* British Petroleum; 707 *t,m* E.T. Archive, *b* Robert Opie Collection; 708 Bettmann Archive; 709 Bettmann Archive; 710 Wiener Library/ Bergen-Belsen Memorial Press; 712 Imperial War Museum; 715 Imperial War Museum; 716 E.T. Archive; 717 Frank Spooner Pictures/FERRY; 720 Panos Pictures; 721 *t* TRIP/Eye Ubiquitous, *bl* Camera Press, *br* ZEFA; 722 Camera Press; 723 Hulton-Deutsch Collection; 24 NASA; 726 Camera Press; 727 *t* Hulton-Deutsch Collection, *b* Camera Press; 728 ZEFA; 729 B.N.T.O.; 730 Popperfoto; 73 Camera Press; 732 *t* Frank Spooner Pictures/GAMMA, *b* Hulton-Deutsch Collection; 734 Camera Press; 735 *t* Associated Press, *b* ZEFA; 736 Camera Press; 737 Camera Press; 738 Frank Spooner Pictures/GAMMA; 739 *t* TRIP/Eye Ubiquitous, *b* Frank Spooner Pictures/GAMMA; 740 ZEFA; 74 ZEFA; 74 Camera Press; 743 *t* Live Aid *m* Associated Press, *b* Panos Pictures; 744 NHPA/Martin Wendler; 745 *t* ZEFA, *m* NHPA/K. Ghani, Frank Spooner Pictures/GAMMA.

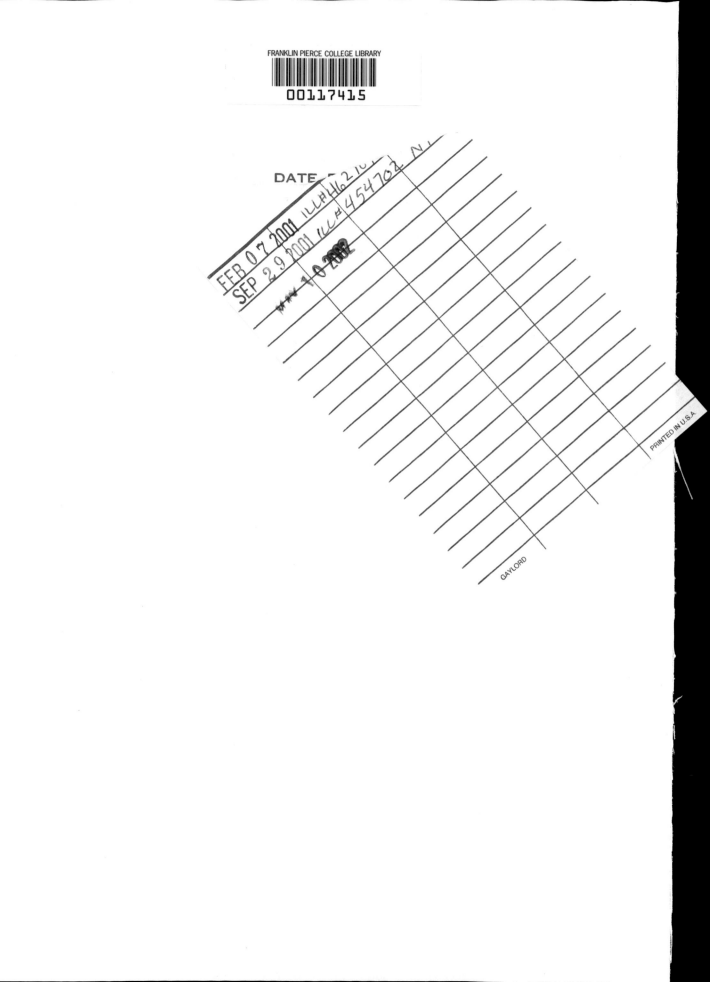